Geoff Tibballs is the author of numerous best-selling humour titles. He is also a keen and very experienced gardener; tireless, too, in the preservation of frogs and newts in his garden.

Other titles

The Little Book of Popular Perennials
Why Can't My Garden Look Like That?
Start and Run a Gardening Business
Plants and Planting Plans for a Bee Garden
30 Herbs for Your Kitchen Garden

100 Plants that Won't Die in Your Garden

Geoff Tibballs

ROBINSON

First published in Great Britain in 2016 by
Robinson

A CIP catalogue record for this book
is available from the British Library.

ISBN 978-1-47213-801-9

Typeset in Sentinel Light by
Hewer Text UK Ltd, Edinburgh
Printed and bound in Great Britain by
CPI Group (UK) Ltd, Croydon CRO 4YY

Papers used by Robinson are from well-
managed forests and other responsible
sources

Robinson
An imprint of
Little, Brown Book Group
Carmelite House
50 Victoria Embankment
London EC4Y 0DZ

An Hachette UK Company
www.hachette.co.uk

www.littlebrown.co.uk

Contents

Introduction

Stocking a garden with plants can be an expensive business, so there are few things more frustrating than when the prized specimen for which you have paid a king's ransom either online or at a garden centre shrivels up and dies within a year or so of purchase. If you can prove that the plant was half-dead when it arrived, you may able to obtain a refund from some online retailers, but for the most part you have to put it down to experience and make a firm mental note not to buy fussy plants in future.

The problem is that many websites and catalogues claim that everything they stock is easy to grow. Herbaceous perennials are a particular minefield. Too often you are told that a certain plant 'will come back year after year' without fail, when in reality it is either so tender that the only chance of it surviving an average British winter is in a greenhouse, or it is a short-lived perennial that is unlikely to flourish beyond two years anyway – and even then only if the local slugs and snails are on a diet.

This book cuts through the horticultural sales pitches by listing 100 plants which, for little care, can reliably be expected to thrive in just about any garden. These plants are all but indestructible – pests give them a wide berth, they will prosper in any reasonable garden soil and will withstand anything that the UK climate throws at them. The key to success in the garden is at planting time. Provided you put these plants in the right spot and remember to water them in thoroughly, you should be assured of year-round colour and interest in your garden for many years to come – and all for the minimum of effort.

Divided into sections for herbaceous perennials, alpines and rockery plants, bulbs, annuals and biennials, grasses, conifers, shrubs, and climbers, and with each entry having a value for money (VFM) rating out of 10, this easy-to-use guide includes the full Latin name of each plant, which you can then use to search for colour images online.

When it comes to buying plants, try to avoid paying more for a plant just because it is in a larger pot. Garden centres and online retailers will often charge £9 or more for a perennial in a 2-litre pot, but if you can find the same plant in a 1-litre or 9cm container you can save a lot of money. It will simply be a younger, less-established specimen, which means that you might have to wait a year for it to flower. But gardening is not all about instant results; part of the joy is in acquiring small plants and watching them grow until, under your expertise, they flourish year after year. The great thing about all the plants I have listed here is that they demand very little of that expertise, which allows you more time to carry out the really important duties in the garden – relaxing in a chair with a cold beer or a glass of wine, the lord or lady of all you survey.

The 12-step guide to planting

The plants listed in this book are tough, but even they will struggle to thrive in the hands of a gardener who just lobs them into the ground and hopes for the best. Planting time is the most important stage of any garden plant's life. Give them a good start and they should do well; with bad preparation they may decide to give up the battle.

Here are the twelve steps to successful planting:

1 Water the plant well the day before planting.

2 Dig a hole that is twice the width of, and a few inches deeper than, the pot in which the plant is currently growing. If planting a bare-root specimen (i.e. no pot), make sure the hole is wide and deep enough for the roots to be spread out.

3 Remove any large stones or other obstructions from the hole.

4 Scatter a 2in or 3in layer of multi-purpose compost in the bottom of the hole so that the roots will have something soft to grow into.

5 Add a couple of handfuls of fertiliser in line with the directions on the box; the bigger the plant, the more fertiliser it will need. With large plants, such as herbaceous border perennials, shrubs and trees, it is also a good idea to add some rotted garden compost or manure to the soil before planting, to get them off to a good start. You can buy a large bag of ready-packed farmyard manure from a garden centre for about £5.

6   Add a layer of horticultural grit to the mixture in the bottom of the hole to improve drainage (especially if your soil is heavy clay). You can buy a large bag of horticultural grit from a garden centre for about £6, and that should last you all summer.

7   Remove the plant from its pot by gently squeezing the sides and tapping the base. Don't worry if the tips of the roots are growing through the drainage holes in the base of the pot and have to be left behind – the root ball is obviously so well established that it can bear to lose a few strays. Tease the roots through the holes or, if it's a plastic pot, cut through the pot without damaging the route system.

8   If the plant appears pot-bound (i.e. the roots are squashed in tightly), gently loosen a few of the roots at the sides and bottom of the root ball without breaking them.

9   Place the plant carefully in the centre of the hole. With the exception of bulbs (which will be covered in the relevant section), the crown of the plant – whether you are dealing with a container-grown plant or a bare-root specimen – should be at soil level. Too deep and it may rot in winter; too shallow and you risk frost damage.

10 Fill the spaces at the sides of the planting hole with multi-purpose compost.

11 With trees, shrubs and roses, carefully tread the soil around the plant with your feet to ensure that it is firmly in the ground. With smaller plants such as perennials, you can use your hands. Where the soil has been firmed down, top up with loose soil or compost so that the crown is once again

at ground level. On no account should any roots be visible above ground.

12 Water the plant in thoroughly – the larger the plant, the more water it will need. Unless it rains steadily in the meantime, water again for the next couple of days.

PART I

Herbaceous perennials

A perennial is a plant that comes back year after year and therefore represents excellent value for money. This section deals with herbaceous perennials which, as a rule, die down every winter before producing fresh shoots the following spring. However, a few – such as hellebores – remain evergreen right through winter. Unless stated otherwise, it is advisable to cut down the stems of herbaceous perennials to the ground in late autumn so that they can return with renewed vigour in spring.

Some species of perennial are short-lived, unreliably hardy in the UK, slug magnets, notoriously fussy about soil conditions and need lifting and dividing regularly to prevent deterioration. However, there are no border divas listed here – the plants I have selected can be relied upon to perform year after year in any reasonable garden soil, are not prone to pests, can largely be left undisturbed and are as tough as old boots.

Achillea millefolium 'Lilac Beauty' (Yarrow)

The achillea (or yarrow) is a popular perennial for the middle of the border, producing flat heads composed of dozens of small, tightly packed flowers above clumps of fragrant, ferny foliage. The colour range is impressive (from white through yellow and terracotta to deep wine-red) but tends to deteriorate (some disappearing altogether) after a few years.

An exception is *A. millefolium* **'Lilac Beauty'**, which produces long-lasting, lilac-pink flowers on upright 3ft stems above a carpet of dark green leaves for up to three months in the height of summer. Although garden guides will tell you that it spreads to no more than 18in, if left to its own devices it will rapidly spread over 5–6ft by means of its shallow, creeping rhizomes, and scatter fast-growing seedlings over a far greater distance. Since it swallows up every other plant in its path, you need to give it plenty of space. This plant is invasive, but in a good way, and its soothing drift of pink compensates for any thuggish behaviour, particularly when set near (but not too near) dark-red roses. If you want to restrict its progress, simply dig up the seedlings and either throw them away or plant them in another part of the garden where space is not at a premium. It thrives in any soil but, like all yarrows, needs a sunny location. As the plant gets bigger, the outer sections may need some support to stop it flopping in the middle.

Likes Reasonably drained soil in full sun.
Flowering season June–September.
Key points Self-seeds vigorously, long flowering season.
VFM 7

Aconitum (Monkshood)

No border perennial is as stately as the delphinium, but it has an alarming tendency to die off in winter in heavy soils. Even if you are lucky enough to find new shoots poking through in spring, you can be sure that the neighbourhood slugs and snails have spotted them too. It is not easy to find a trouble-free alternative that produces similarly elegant spires of blue, but the aconitum comes pretty close. But before you get too excited, there is one important thing to remember, particularly if you have children: every part of the aconitum plant is highly **poisonous**, so you should always wear gloves when handling it and make sure that it is planted towards the back of the border far away from inquisitive young hands. Its toxicity is not all bad news, however, for it means that even the hungriest of slugs and snails give aconitum leaves a wide berth.

Its common name of monkshood derives from the racemes of helmet-shaped flowers that resemble sinister, cowled hoods and are carried on tall, upright stems. The deeply cut foliage can appear as early as February, but although some reach a height of 6ft, the clump does not spread to much more than 2ft. Ideally the aconitum genus prefer a semi-shaded spot, but they will tolerate full sun provided the soil remains moist. So if you do put it in a sunny location, add plenty of well-rotted organic matter when planting and remember to water regularly in dry weather. To reduce the risk of them drying out, mulch by spreading a thick layer of rotted organic matter (such as leaf mould or garden compost) around the base of the plants in spring. Mulching not only retains moisture, it also suppresses weeds and improves the soil by releasing nutrients.

Most species of aconitum flower in early or mid-summer, but a few bloom much later – in September – so by planting a selection you can have a monkshood in bloom for months on end. Be aware that the plants die off very quickly after flowering, but that doesn't mean there is anything wrong. However, it does mean that you need to make a mental note of where they are to prevent you accidentally digging up the rhizomes when planting bulbs in autumn. While blue is the most common colour, you can also buy white and pink forms. The flowers may not quite match the majesty or the subtle shades of delphiniums (to which they are related), but they are definitely worth a try. Here are some of the best:

A. **'Bressingham Spire'** is a good blue to choose if you don't want anything too tall. Its violet-blue flowers appear on 3ft stems and it will eventually form a clump covering a width of 18in. June–Aug.

A. cammarum **'Bicolour'** has glossy, dark-green leaves and spectacular spikes of blue and white flowers, the colours merging together like a tie-dye T-shirt. This is an excellent cultivar for those looking for something different in the garden. It reaches a height of 4ft and a spread of 18in. June–Aug. *A. cammarum* **'Pink Sensation'** has soft pink flowers on stems up to 4ft high. June–Aug.

A. carmichaelii **'Arendsii'** is a lovely autumn-flowering monkshood that produces deep-blue flowers above attractive broad leaves that are tinged with red when young. Height 5ft, spread 2ft. Aug–Oct. *A. carmichaelii* **'Royal Flush'** is a shorter species but an equally intense blue, with a height of 2ft and a spread of 1ft. Aug–Oct.

A. napellus **'Gletschereis'** has large white flowers carried above glossy green leaves. It is one of the more compact cultivars, reaching a height of 3ft and a spread of 18in. May–June.

A. **'Spark's Variety'** has rich, deep-violet-blue flowers and an abundance of flowering side stems. It reaches a height of 6ft and a spread of 2ft, making it an excellent specimen for the back of a narrow border. June–Aug.

A. **'Stainless Steel'** has unusual but highly effective grey-blue flowers touched with creamy white. As such, it makes a good contrast when planted alongside the darker blue aconitums or against a dark background. It reaches a height of 4ft and a spread of 18in. June–Aug.

Likes Partial shade, moist soil.

Flowering season Summer or autumn according to variety.

Key points Good on clay soil, easy to maintain, a trouble-free, slug-proof alternative to delphiniums. All parts of the plant are highly poisonous, so always wear gloves when handling it and keep the plant well away from children. Warn anyone of any age who is likely to go near the plant of its dangers.

VFM 7

Ajuga reptans 'Burgundy Glow' (Bugle)

This garden form of the familiar wild bugle could never be described as the most eye-catching plant, but its deep-pink evergreen foliage, with attractive grey-green splashes and cream edging plus short spires of deep-blue flowers, contrasts well with miniature daffodils in spring. It only grows to a height of 6in but spreads rapidly, creeping between bulbs and taller plants to form a dense carpet with a width of 2 or 3ft. It prefers a moist location with a fair amount of shade (the leaves will scorch in full sun) and is therefore a useful plant for trailing along the side of a pond. It is hardy, undemanding (growing in even the poorest of soils), and will often seed itself so that small clumps of bugle can be found sprouting up in the vicinity, especially in a boggy spot where few other plants will flourish. Although the flowering season lasts no more than a few weeks, the leaves keep their colour right through summer and into autumn, developing bronze and wine-red tones.

It needs no care whatsoever other than cutting back if it becomes too invasive and will live happily undisturbed in the garden for years. All cultivars of *Ajuga reptans* are equally reliable, including *A. reptans* **'Black Scallop'**, which has leaves with centres that are almost black.

Likes Moisture-retentive soil in a shady spot.
Flowering season April–May.
Key points Good groundcover plant, attractive pink foliage throughout summer, fast growing – even in poor soil.
VFM 6

Alchemilla mollis (Lady's Mantle)

Lady's mantle takes its botanical name of *Alchemilla mollis* from the Arabic for 'little magical one' because it was believed in ancient times that the water collected from its leaves following a morning dew possessed healing properties. The plant certainly looks at its best when its soft, hairy, pale-green leaves are sparkling with dewdrops, but it also throws up sprays of tiny yellow-green flowers in summer, a combination that makes it popular with flower arrangers. If it is cut back hard after flowering in August, it will often produce a second flush. It is unfussy about soil conditions – thriving in everything from sand to heavy clay – and will grow in sun or partial shade, quickly reaching a height and spread of 18in. It will also self-seed freely.

By itself it may not be the most spectacular specimen in the garden, but a group of three planted next to blue hardy geraniums makes for a pleasing colour combination for the front of a border. Allow it to spill over onto paths so that its leaves soften the edges.

Likes Any soil in sun or partial shade.
Flowering season June–August.
Key points Pretty apple-green leaves, grows in any soil, good for groundcover, self-seeds.
VFM 6

Anaphalis (Pearly Everlasting)

This hardy perennial is grown for its silver-grey foliage and its attractive heads of small, white, papery, daisy-like flowers that can be dried for winter decoration. Even when cut and dried, the colour and texture of the flower remain intact, which is why it is sometimes known as the pearly everlasting flower. It will grow in any reasonably drained soil that does not completely dry out in summer, performing well even in poor ground, and although it prefers full sun, it will tolerate partial shade.

The most commonly available species, *Anaphalis triplinervis*, will quickly reach a height and spread of 2ft. A popular cultivar is *A. triplinervis* **'Sommerschnee'**, which has pure white flowers fitting for its English translation of 'Summer Snow'. You may also find *Anaphalis margaritacea var. yedoensis*, which produces straight stems up to 2ft 6in tall topped by clusters of small, white flowers with yellow centres.

Likes Reasonably drained soil in sun or partial shade.

Flowering season August–October.

Key points Everlasting flowers, good for cutting and drying. Silver-grey foliage.

VFM 6

Aquilegia (Columbine)

Unless you are careful, May can be a bit of a quiet month in terms of garden colour. The spring bulbs have mostly finished and the summer flowers are still waiting to burst into bloom, but one plant fills that void with style and elegance: the columbine. It is also popularly known as 'Granny's Bonnet' for the jaunty, hat-like shape of the nodding flowers on that old cottage-garden favourite, *Aquilegia vulgaris*. The genus name *Aquilegia* is derived from the Latin word for eagle (*aquila*) because the petals on the long-spurred forms are said to resemble an eagle's claw.

Whichever form you grow, the flowers will be unrivalled in their daintiness and also in the sheer range of colour combinations, covering almost every shade imaginable from pure white to black. Many cultivars feature more than one colour, mixing red and yellow, red and white or navy blue and white. The greygreen, ferny leaves are beautiful in their own right, and it is also possible to find ones with variegated foliage. They may appear delicate, but columbines are surprisingly tough, hardy enough to cope with any UK winter. The only thing they will not survive is badly waterlogged soil. Since they appreciate good drainage, add plenty of horticultural grit if you garden on clay. They prefer a spot in partial shade but will tolerate full sun provided you give them a thick mulch in spring and water them in times of drought.

Border aquilegias reach a height of around 3ft with a 1ft spread. The only downside is that they are not as long-lived as some other herbaceous perennials, but you can still expect to get four or five flowering years out of them. In any case they self-seed with such abandon that for every parent plant you will find half a dozen offspring naturalising themselves nearby, perpetuating the line. These do not always come true to type, but part of the excitement is wondering what the new 'baby' will be: inky blue, mauve or even chocolate-brown. Whatever it is, you will not be disappointed for there is no such thing as a boring aquilegia. To encourage seed dispersion, leave one or two of the flower heads on each plant after it has finished blooming. (Leaving all the old heads on will use up a lot of the plant's energy and as a result you will probably get fewer flowers on the parent plant the following year.) Alternatively, collect the green seed-pods and store them until they turn brown. The mature seeds will now be black and you can simply scatter them around the garden in late summer or autumn and wait for new seedlings to appear the following spring, although they will not flower in that first year.

The easiest – and certainly the cheapest – way to start a collection of columbines is to sow a packet of seeds, such as mixed McKana Giant Hybrids, a form famed for its rich array of colours, large flowers and long spurs, or Winky Mixture, an assortment of shorter (2ft tall) doubles with mauve, blue or red flowers (many with white centres) that face upwards rather than horizontally. Even if you usually struggle to get seedlings to germinate, columbines are really reliable. Just follow the instructions on the packet. You can, of course, buy small plants. Sometimes these will just be labelled 'mixed' or, if you are happy to spend a little more, look out for some of these named cultivars:

A. chrysantha **'Yellow Queen'** has exquisite, primrose-yellow flowers with long spurs.

A. vulgaris **'Adelaide Addison'** is a lovely double form with dark-blue outer petals while the inner petals are white edged with blue. *A. vulgaris* **'Crimson Star'** has scarlet-red outer petals and inner petals that are white with a red centre. *A. vulgaris* **'William Guiness'** (aka **'Magpie'**) has unusual purple-black outer petals and inner petals that are white edged purple-black.

A. vulgaris var. stellata features the Barlow series, which have beautiful, double, spur-less flower heads around a cluster of yellow stamens. Seek out **'Black Barlow'** (black), **'Blue Barlow'** (inky blue), **'Nora Barlow'** (pink with white tips) and **'White Barlow'** (white). *A. vulgaris var. stellata* **'Ruby Port'** has double, spur-less burgundy flowers.

Likes Well-drained soil in sun or partial shade.

Flowering season May–June.

Key points Beautiful, delicate flowers in a huge array of colours, shapes and styles. Quintessential cottage-garden plant, self-seeds freely to give you extra plants.

VFM 9

Astilbe

With its large plume-like flowers in red, pink or white rising above glossy, finely cut foliage, astilbe is one of the most attractive plants for a shady or semi-shaded spot in the garden. It is also one of the easiest, provided you dig in plenty of rotted organic matter at planting time, add a thick layer of mulch in spring to retain moisture, and water thoroughly in dry weather. The flowering period is summer, but when the feathery blooms have finished, instead of dropping they retain their shape and turn golden to mid-brown. These are by no means ugly, so instead of deadheading (as is the norm with most border perennials), leave the spent flowers in place to provide interest well into the autumn. You can finally cut off the dead flowers as late as November, along with the leaves.

Most astilbes reach a height of between 2 and 3ft and form a neat clump measuring about 18in across. They do not need supporting and their love of moist soil makes them excellent specimens for a bog garden or the edge of a pond. Here are a few of the best astilbes to grow:

A. chinensis **'Look At Me'** carries masses of delicate pink flowers on red stalks above grey-green, fern-like foliage. Height 2ft. July–Aug. The dwarf *A. chinensis* **'Pumila'** has spikes of rosy-mauve flowers and grows to a height of only 1ft. July–Aug. *A. chinensis* **'Vision in Red'** is a taller form (3ft) and bears plumes of pink-purple flowers above a mound of green leaves that are tinged with red. July–Aug.

A. **'Fanal'** (× *arendsii*) has bronze emerging shoots that turn a rich, emerald green and are followed by delightful deep-red flowers. Height 2ft. June–July.

A. japonica **'Europa'** produces soft, fluffy, shell-pink flowers above glossy green leaves. Height 2ft. June–July.

A. thunbergii **'Professor van der Wielen'** has white flowers on upright stems that reach nearly 3ft and mid-green leaves. July–Aug.

Likes Some shade, moist soil.

Flowering season June–August (depending on variety).

Key points Pretty, feathery flowers and attractive leaves. Good for clay, long season of interest.

VFM 7

Bergenia (Elephant's Ears)

You might expect a plant whose common name is elephant's ears to be tough, and the bergenia does not disappoint. It gets its name from its large, leathery, evergreen leaves, which start out bright green before turning wine-red in late autumn and winter, thereby providing invaluable colour at a time when the garden can otherwise look decidedly barren. Above the leaves in early spring rise sturdy stems bearing pretty hyacinth-like flowers in shades from magenta-pink through to white. It happily grows in sun or partial shade, in any type of soil, and is particularly useful for planting under trees as it is able to withstand dry conditions. It is the essence of low-maintenance gardening, requiring nothing more than deadheading after flowering and the removal of any damaged leaves. It will reach a height and spread of 18in, and any clumps that become too big can be lifted and divided in autumn.

This old cottage-garden favourite fell out of favour for a while but has enjoyed something of a renaissance thanks to the introduction of a number of new cultivars. These include **'Bach'** (white flowers that age to a blush pink), **'Ballawley'** (large rose-red flowers on red stems), **'Bressingham White'** (a shorter, 12in cultivar with white flowers), **'Bressingham Ruby'** (deep rose-red flowers and excellent autumn foliage colour), **'Overture'** (magenta flowers carried on scarlet stems and outstanding winter colour), and **'Pink Dragonfly'** (coral-pink flowers which repeat in mid-summer and provide good autumn colour).

Likes Any soil in sun or partial shade.
Flowering season March–April.
Key points Unfussy about soil, good autumn foliage colour, provides year-round interest. Low maintenance, extremely robust.
VFM 7

Brunnera macrophylla (Siberian Bugloss)

This easy-to-grow little perennial produces 20in sprays of deep-blue forget-me-not flowers in spring to complement daffodils and hellebores. It likes a spot with at least partial shade and is ideal for planting under trees in a woodland garden; for although it prefers moist soil, once established it will tolerate periods of drought. The rough, heart-shaped leaves form dense mounds but spread to no more than 18in. If you can find it, seek out *B. macrophylla* **'Jack Frost'**, which has the added bonus of attractive silver variegated leaves that are edged and veined with green and contrast well with its blue flowers. Even when the flowers have finished, the foliage continues to look good alongside summer perennials, thus providing an extended period of interest and greater value for money. This and other variegated brunneras need deep shade and a more sheltered spot than those with plain green foliage in order to prevent strong winds scorching the leaves.

Arranged in groups of three or more, brunnera makes a good groundcover plant for what can be a difficult location.

Likes Any soil in a shady location.
Flowering season April–May.
Key points Blue spring flowers, variegated leaves. Good for planting under trees.
VFM 7

Centaurea montana (Cornflower)

The perennial cornflower will offer many years of colour provided your soil does not become waterlogged in winter. Given reasonable drainage and a sunny location (although it can cope with light shade), it will quickly spread even on poor soil, its soft grey-green leaves appearing in February followed by flowers in white, pink, lilac, blue or deep purple in late spring. These open from thistle-like buds, and the large, 2in-wide, spidery flower heads have contrasting centres. For example, the most commonly available type, the blue, has a violet-purple centre. In hot, dry summers, the leaves can be affected by mildew, but in any case it is a good idea to cut all the foliage – diseased or not – right back to the ground after flowering in the hope of inducing a second crop of flowers. It grows to a height of 18in and will cover a width of up to 2ft. If the clumps threaten to outgrow their allotted space, they can be divided every few years in spring, which will also help to rejuvenate the plant.

A new cultivar to look out for is *C. montana* **'Jordy'**, which does not spread as rapidly as some perennial cornflowers but has flowers in an unusual dark plum-purple. These look particularly effective when planted in conjunction with the white cornflower, *C. montana* **'Alba'**, or the lilac-pink *C. montana* **'Carnea'**.

Likes Reasonably drained soil in a sunny spot.
Flowering season May–July.
Key points Good colour range, long-lived, will grow in poor soil.
VFM 7

Echinops ritro 'Veitch's Blue' (Globe Thistle)

The echinops – or globe thistle – takes its name from its dark-blue, globular flower heads and grey-green, thistle-like leaves. Both the dead flower heads and the leaves can be decidedly prickly, so it is a plant best handled with gardening gloves. Other than staking, that is pretty much the only care it requires as it will grow happily on any soil – even poor or chalky ground – so long as the drainage is adequate (in other words, no winter waterlogging) and it receives plenty of sunshine. Given these conditions, it will readily produce a succession of 3in-wide blooms on 3ft-tall stiff stems during late summer year after year.

With its leaves providing interest from spring onwards, it is a useful specimen for the middle or back of a border, where the flowers prove particularly attractive to butterflies and bees and where the ball-shaped flowers contrast well with daisies and tall spires. Alternatively, if a few of the blooms are cut before they have completely opened, they can be taken indoors as a cut flower or dried for later use in an arrangement. The stems should be cut down to the ground anyway after flowering to encourage a second flush of blooms. It is not a plant that takes up much room at ground level, spreading to no more than 18in.

Likes Reasonably drained soil in full sun.

Flowering season July–September.

Key points Will grow in poor soil, stately blue flowers, good for flower arrangements. Attracts butterflies and bees.

VFM 7

Erigeron speciosus (Fleabane)

Don't be put off by its common name – the erigeron is a serious contender for the front of a border, where it produces pretty, often double, Michaelmas-daisy-like flowers but much earlier in the season. The best types to grow are members of *E. speciosus,* which, in mid-summer, produce large, flat, daisy flowers in pink, lilac or dark violet with contrasting yellow centres that freely attract butterflies, bees and other insects. All varieties reach a height of 2ft and a spread of 1ft, but the slender stems do have a tendency to flop if they are not supported. They will grow in any soil with reasonable drainage, are drought tolerant, and like plenty of sun, although they can cope with some light shade. If the centre of the plant starts to deteriorate after a few years, the plant can be lifted, the dying section discarded, and the healthy sections replanted.

E. speciosus **'Dunkelste Aller'** (**'Darkest of All'**) was bred in Germany and has delightful semi-double, dark-violet flowers, which really stand out next to their yellow centres. Its fellow countryman, *E. speciosus* **'Foerster's Liebling'**, has semi-double, carmine-pink flowers, while *E. speciosus* **'Pink Jewel'** has paler, lilac-pink, semi-double flowers. There is also a tough erigeron for rockery duty (see Alpines p.70).

Likes Reasonably drained soil in sun or light shade.
Flowering season June–August.
Key points Drought tolerant, attracts butterflies and bees.
VFM 6

Geranium (Cranesbill)

Of all perennials, no genus is more diverse, reliable and therefore invaluable for the gardener seeking guaranteed success than the hardy geranium or cranesbill, its common name stemming from the long, beak-like seed capsule which many species possess. With well over three hundred types to choose from in a colour range from whites through pinks and blues to purple and almost black, including many with ornate veining, hardy geraniums are a must for any border or cottage garden. Apart from the dwarf *G. cinereum*, which requires particularly well-drained soil and is therefore not included here, the other readily available hardy geraniums will grow in any soil that does not become waterlogged, are untroubled by pests and diseases, and there are species for every position from full sun to deep shade. If you cut the plant back hard after the first flush of flowers, you will often be rewarded with a second flush in late summer or early autumn. Many forms provide excellent ground cover, but there are also species that grow to a height of over 3ft, making hardy geraniums the most versatile of garden plants. The blues, in particular, are ideal companions for roses.

Here are some of the choicest hardy geraniums:

G. **'Blue Cloud'** carries a cascade of large sky-blue flowers with violet veins for months on end which look spectacular when planted near orange geums. A vigorous grower in full sun or partial shade, it can reach a height of 3ft and a spread of over 5ft, and just when you think it has finally stopped flowering, it comes back for more. To encourage a second flush, cut it back hard in August. **June–Oct.**

G. clarkei **'Kashmir Purple'** has relatively large violet-pink flowers over a vigorous-growing clump of finely divided foliage. It can be cut back after flowering to produce a second flush. Happy in sun or partial shade, it reaches a height of 18in and a spread of 2ft 6in. **June–Sept.** The white version, *G. clarkei* **'Kashmir White'**, has beautiful white flowers with lilac veins. It is less vigorous than its purple cousin, reaching a height of 18in and a spread of 1ft. If cut back after flowering, you may be rewarded with a second crop. June–Sept.

G. *himalayense* **'Plenum'** is a real beauty with delightful double mauve flowers in early summer and repeated later in the season. Growing to a height of 10in and with a spread of 2ft, it is unfussy and is easily multiplied by digging up the outer sections of the plant. The double pompom flowers set this apart from other geraniums and the intense colour is one that is otherwise not readily found in the garden. It grows best in sun or partial shade, and because (unlike its single cousins) it does not self-seed, it will flower over a long period. May–Sept.

G. **'Johnson's Blue'** has long been one of the most popular hardy cranesbills. The large lavender-blue flowers that become paler at the centre are produced earlier than most other blues and it will repeat if cut back after the first flush. Happy in sun or light shade, it has an informal habit and will quickly establish itself to a height of 18in and a spread of at least 2ft. May–Aug.

G. **'Light Dilys'** is a charming little geranium that bears lilac-pink flowers with a maroon eye and maroon veining right through summer. It also has attractive leaves, which in autumn turn from light green to a glowing orange-red. It will grow in sun or partial shade and reaches a height of 1ft and a spread of 18in. June–Oct.

G. *macrorrhizum* **'Ingwersen's Variety'** is a low-growing, rhizomatous plant with small pale-pink petals and contrasting deep-pink sepals produced in abundance above a dense clump of highly aromatic green and red foliage. Happy in sun or full shade, it grows to about 1ft high but will soon spread to 4ft or more, making it an excellent groundcover specimen for suppressing weeds. G. *macrorrhizum* **'Czakor'** has darker, magenta-pink flowers, while G. *macrorrhizum* **'White-Ness'** has pure white flowers. All flower May–June.

G. *magnificum* **'Rosemoor'** has clumps of hairy leaves and masses of large, warm, deep-violet flowers with darker veins. It grows to a height of 18in with a spread of 2ft, making it ideal for the front of a border. Although it will cope with light shade, it prefers full sun. May–June.

G. **'Nimbus'** has medium-large, lilac-blue flowers with red veining and a small white centre that are produced above a mound of attractive dissected leaves. The foliage is yellow-green in spring before turning green in summer. It will grow in sun or partial shade, reaches a height and spread of 2ft and will provide a second flush of blooms if cut back after flowering. June–Sept.

G. *nodosum* **'Clos du Coudray'** has one of the most distinctive flowers of any hardy geranium: a rich, veined lilac-purple with darker blotches and paler edges. The blooms are produced above a mass of dark, glossy, maple-like leaves right through summer and well into late autumn, when the leaves turn a dazzling red. It grows to 15in high with a similar spread, is equally happy in sun or full shade and seeds itself profusely. June–Oct. G. *nodosum* **'Svelte Lilac'** bears heavily veined lilac flowers, even in deep shade and dry positions. Height and spread 15in. June–Oct.

G. **'Orion'** is an excellent violet-blue with large flowers carried on wiry stems over a long period. It grows to 2ft 6in in height, with a similar spread, and the finely divided leaves turn red in autumn. It grows quickly and is happy in full sun or partial shade. June–Oct.

G. *oxonianum* **'Lace Time'** bears trumpet-shaped white flowers with dark pink veins in a pattern so intricate and delicate that each petal appears to have been hand-painted by an accomplished artist. Happy in full sun or partial shade, it blooms from late spring and will repeat if cut back after flowering. It will quickly grow to a height of 18in and a spread of 2ft or more, making an excellent groundcover plant, and is also an abundant self-seeder, giving you dozens of plants for the price of one. May–Oct. For a rosier pink, choose G. *oxonianum* **'Claridge Druce'**, although because of its darker background its markings are less pronounced. May–Oct. Another popular cultivar is G. *oxonianum* **'Wargrave Pink'**, a vigorous grower that bears an abundance of salmon-pink flowers. This too will produce a second flush if cut back in mid-summer. **May–Oct.**

G. phaeum – 'Mourning Widow' – is an excellent species for a deep shady position in the garden, although it is also perfectly content in full sun, growing quickly to a height of 2ft 6in and a spread of 2ft above a mound of unusual blotched leaves. If the clump becomes too big, it is easily divided in spring. *G. phaeum* **'Samobor'** has burgundy-black flowers, *G. phaeum* **'Raven'** has purple-black flowers, while *G. phaeum* **'Album'** is pure white. The flowers on these are relatively small, so if you are looking for something showier try *G. phaeum* **'Lily Lovell'**, which has slightly larger dusky purple flowers. **May–June.**

G. pratense **'Striatum'** (also known as **'Splish Splash'**) is an eye-catching cultivar with white flowers that are randomly splashed, spotted and striped with violet-blue so that no two flowers on a plant are exactly the same. It reaches a height of 2ft with a 2ft spread and is best in sun or partial shade. **June–July.** A taller plant, growing up to 3ft and with a similar spread, is the vigorous *G. pratense* **'Mrs Kendall Clark'**, which produces a mass of attractively veined, grey-blue saucer-shaped flowers in early summer. It will thrive in sun or partial shade. **May–June.** *G. pratense* **'Summer Skies'** also reaches 3ft in height but has smaller double flowers that are lilac with a white centre. Once established, it blooms profusely in sun or partial shade. **May–Sept.** *G. pratense* **'Plenum Violaceum'** is another double, whose violet-blue, rosebud-like flowers are borne on 2ft stems with a 2ft spread. It is happy in sun or partial shade. **June–Sept.** *G. pratense* **'Plenum Double Jewel'** has double white flowers with a striking purple centre, an exciting new colour break in hardy geraniums. It grows to 18in with a similar spread and will grow in sun or partial shade. **May–July.** If you're looking for something different, try *G. pratense* **'Hocus Pocus'**, a compact form which has single blue flowers and dark purple – almost black – leaves. It reaches a height of 1ft and a spread of 18in and thrives in sun or partial shade. **June–July.**

All tall cultivars of *Geranium pratense* may need some support to prevent the stems flopping.

G. psilostemon, the Armenian cranesbill, produces a mass of vivid magenta-pink flowers with black centres and veins on a fast-growing plant that can reach a height and spread of 4ft. It will grow in full sun or light shade and the leaves turn a brilliant red in autumn. June–Aug. **'Patricia' (=Brempat)** is a hybrid of *G. psilostemon* that is less rambling (height and spread 3ft) and has larger and equally striking magenta and black flowers. June–Aug. Another *G. psilostemon* hybrid to look out for is **'Dragon Heart'**, which grows to about 2ft tall but spreads for over 4ft and has huge magenta and black flowers that measure 2in across. A truly spectacular plant for sun or light shade. June–Aug.

G. renardii has attractive velvety grey-green leaves and delicate five-petalled flowers. A good species for the front of a border or a large rockery, it reaches a height and spread of 18in and prefers sun or light shade. Add horticultural grit when planting to ensure that drainage is good. *G. renardii* **'Walter Ingwersen'** has white flowers with prominent purple veins. May–June. *G. renardii* **'Philippe Vapelle'** has lilac-blue flowers with purple veins. May–June.

G. **'Sabani Blue' (=Bremigo)** has similar rich violet flowers with darker veining to *G. magnificum* but has the advantage of producing a second flush later in the year if cut back. Happy in sun or light shade, it has a height and spread of around 2ft. May–Sept.

G. **'Salome'** is a useful plant for trailing through shrubs or taller plants as its flowering stems spread out to cover 4ft or more. The flowers themselves are pale lilac with a deep purple eye and purple veining – a lovely combination. It will grow in full sun or partial shade to a height of about 1ft. June–Sept.

G. sanguineum is a low-growing species which thrives in sun or partial shade and forms pretty magenta-pink flowers above neat hummocks of shiny dark-green leaves. It establishes itself quickly, will reach a height of 1ft and a spread of 18in and will look equally at home on a rockery as at the front of a border. *G. sanguineum* **'Album'** has clear white flowers, and *G. sanguineum* **'Striatum'** has pale lilac-pink flowers with darker pink veining. All flower May–June.

G. soboliferum **'Starman'** is a new compact cultivar that will appeal to those looking for something a little different in their hardy geraniums. Its pink flowers with darker crimson blotches are more like the markings you would expect to find on a regal pelargonium. It blooms later in the season than most and also has finely divided leaves, which turn a startling red in autumn. Happy in sun or light shade, 'Starman' reaches a height and spread of no more than 18in. July–Sept.

G. **'Storm Chaser'** is a low-growing cultivar that has pretty pale-pink flowers with deeper magenta veins and centres. The flowers are not large but are produced in abundance on a plant that grows no higher than 10in and spreads about 18in. Bred in the Orkneys, it is happy in sun or partial shade and its compact nature means that it will not overpower its neighbours, making it a good choice for groundcover where space is limited. June–Oct.

G. sylvaticum **'Mayflower'** has small but enchanting violet-blue flowers with a white eye in late spring and early summer. It likes sun or partial shade and grows to a height of 2ft 6in with a spread of 1ft 6in. *G. sylvaticum* **'Amy Doncaster'** is a slightly deeper blue. May–June.

G. wallichianum generally prefers a position that receives a little shade. It does not self-seed, but large clumps can be divided in spring. **'Buxton's Blue'** has saucer-shaped blue flowers with a large white central zone. It grows to a height of 2ft 6in and can spread up to 4ft. July–Oct. **'Rozanne' (=Gerwat)** is a hybrid of 'Buxton's Blue' that was discovered as recently as 1989 but has made such an impact that it was voted Plant of the Centenary at the 2013 Chelsea Flower Show. It has even larger flowers than its parent, making it a real showstopper, and blooms earlier above attractive mottled foliage. If cut back hard in late July, it will produce a fine second flush of flowers in autumn. Height 2ft 6in, spread 4ft. June–Oct. *G. wallichianum* 'Azure Rush' (height 1ft, spread 2ft) is a lower-growing, more compact sport (purposely bred variation) of 'Rozanne' but has flowers that are every bit as large. June–Oct. *G. wallichianum* 'Havana Blues' is another recent introduction that grows to a height of 18in and a spread of 2ft; its huge violet-blue flowers are enhanced by dark veins that radiate out from the white centre. June–Sept. *G. wallichianum* 'Rise and Shine' (height 1ft, spread 4ft) also has large white-eyed blue flowers, but with magenta veins and a prominent magenta ring around the eye. Its lax stems look especially pretty when allowed to trail over a low wall. June–Oct. *G. wallichianum* 'Crystal Lake' has medium-sized pale-lilac flowers with deep purple veins, a most attractive combination. A sprawling plant, it will grow to around 18in tall with a spread of 2ft or more. June–Oct.

G. wlassovianum blooms later in the summer than most other hardy geraniums, but is worth the wait for its lovely violet flowers with darker veining. These are complemented by foliage which emerges pinkish-bronze in spring, turns green in summer and finally a fiery red in autumn. It reaches a height of 18in and will spread to 2ft or more. It is happy in sun or partial shade, but does prefer some moisture in the soil. July–Sept.

Likes Any soil with decent drainage. There are varieties for full sun, partial shade or deep shade.

Flowering season May–September (depending on variety).

Key points Long flowering season, unfussy, will flourish for years without any need to divide. Some self-seed, giving you extra plants for your money.

VFM 10

Geum (Avens)

Orange is one of the most important colours in the garden, capable of lighting up a border even on the dullest day. Until fairly recently there were precious few reliable plants able to provide that dazzling splash of colour, but the ever-expanding range of geums has filled the gap admirably. They cope with any soils – from heavy clay to chalk or sand – and start flowering as early as May. Set among drifts of blue forget-me-nots, orange and tangerine geums form a match made in gardening heaven. They need little attention, although they should be cut back hard at the end of the flowering season to rejuvenate the foliage for the following year. They should also be lifted and divided every four or five years when any weak sections can be discarded. Geums are so hardy that they often remain evergreen through milder UK winters. Here are some of the best varieties:

G. **'Alabama Slammer'** is a spectacular new avens with ruffled, semi-double flowers that are gold with red and orange markings like a colourful cocktail. They are medium-size and are borne on burgundy stems above glossy, light-green leaves. Fast growing, it is best in full sun or light shade and reaches a height and spread of 18in. May–Aug.

G. **'Banana Daiquiri'** has semi-double lemon-yellow flowers with a whirl of yellow anthers at the centre. The flowers appear on lime-green stems. It forms a neat plant for the front of a border or a rockery, growing to a height and spread of around 18in. It likes a sunny spot but will tolerate light shade. May–Aug.

G. **'Blazing Sunset'** is a new, more compact, version of the old favourite 'Mrs J. Bradshaw' (see overleaf), and has the added bonus of large, fully double, scarlet flowers, giving a vibrant splash of hot colour for the summer border. It is happy in full sun or light shade and reaches a height and spread of 2ft. June–Sept.

G. **'Borisii'** is a compact plant (height and spread 1ft) bearing single flowers of fiery orange with prominent yellow stamens above a dense mound of furry green leaves. It prefers a sunny spot – ideally one that retains some moisture in summer – and if deadheaded regularly will flower for many months. **May–Sept.**

G. chiloense **'Dolly North'** is an old cultivar that produces a profusion of magnificent, large, semi-double orange flowers on long stems above a dense mound of hairy leaves from May right through summer. When deadheading, take care not to cut the stems back too far because you may lose some flowering side shoots. It grows to a height and spread of 2ft 6in and, like all geums, needs no staking. Happy in full sun or light shade. **May–Sept.** If you're looking for a red old variety, *G. chiloense* **'Mrs. J. Bradshaw'** is readily obtainable. This can reach a height and spread of nearly 3ft, will grow in sun or light shade and has semi-double scarlet flowers. **June–Aug.** *G. chiloense* **'Lady Stratheden'** has graced gardens for almost a century and produces warm, semi-double yellow flowers on 2ft 6in stems with a similar spread. It will grow in sun or light shade. **June–Aug.** As with all plants, deadhead regularly to prolong the flowering season.

G. coccineum **'Eos'** is a small plant grown more for its refreshing lime-green foliage than its single orange flowers which, by geum standards, are relatively small and sparse. The foliage contrasts well with burgundy-leaved heucheras and, like them, it prefers a spot with a little shade from the afternoon sun. It grows to a height of 9in and a spread of 1ft. **June–Aug.** *G. coccineum* **'Werner Arends'** has standard mid-green foliage but compensates by producing larger, single coppery-orange flowers and in greater numbers. It grows to a height and spread of 16in and will do well in sun or light shade. **June–Sept.**

G. **'Fire Storm'** is a new compact variety bearing large semi-double flowers in a dazzling shade of tangerine with a touch of red at the edges of the petals. These contrast nicely with the dark-green leaves. It likes full sun and reaches a height and spread of just over 1ft. **May–Aug.**

G. **'Mai Tai'** has superb, frilly yellow and pink semi-double flowers that are flushed with apricot to create a peachy hue that is rarely available in garden plants. The flowers, which later fade to a pale-melon colour, emerge from contrasting dark-red buds that are carried on slender, upright stems. It reaches a height and spread of 18in and performs best in full sun, although some shade is tolerated. May–July.

G. **'Mandarin'** produces large, semi-double, bright-orange flowers. It is happy in sun or light shade and will eventually reach a height and spread of 2ft. June–Sept.

G. **'Prinses Juliana'** has semi-double, warm-orange flowers carried on long stems above a mound of green leaves. It likes full sun or light shade and reaches a height and spread of 18in. May–Sept.

G. *rivale*, the water avens, has drooping flower heads that are noticeably smaller and less showy than those on other types of geum. It is happy in sun or partial shade but, as its common name suggests, it does need moisture-retentive soil. G. *rivale* **'Leonard's Variety'** is a clump-forming perennial that produces semi-double coppery-pink flowers on reddish-brown stems. It reaches a height and spread of 18in. May–June.

G. **'Tequila Sunrise'** has distinctive primrose-yellow, semi-double flowers with indiscriminate splashes of apricot orange, an unusual but highly desirable colour combination. These are carried on slender dark-red stems above the hairy, mid-green leaves. It likes a sunny location and will reach a height and spread of 18in. May–Aug.

G. **'Totally Tangerine'** is an outstanding recent introduction that produces a wealth of large, cheerful, single tangerine flowers over a long period. It prefers a sunny spot, where it will reach a height and spread of 18in. May–Aug.

Likes Any soil in sun or light shade.
Flowering season May–September (depending on variety).
Key points Valuable source of orange flowers in the garden, will prosper in any soil, easy care.
VFM 10

Helleborus (Hellebore)

In December and January, when the garden is otherwise at its bleak-est, hellebores come into their own, delivering closely packed groups of large, saucer-shaped flowers in shades of white, lime green, pink, red, purple, and almost black. Some varieties are flamboyant doubles, some have anemone-type centres with a dense cluster of half-formed petals in the middle, while others have ornate blotched markings on the inside of the flower. Since the flowers often hang down, these beautiful patterns sometimes only become visible when you lift the heads for closer inspection.

They last for months – right up until late spring – and need very little care. They prefer a spot with some shade – ideally close to the house so that you can enjoy them in the depths of winter without having to venture outside – and prefer moisture-retentive soil, so add plenty of organic matter or leaf mould when planting, give them an annual spring mulch, and water in periods of drought. The large leaves are a handsome glossy green with uncompromising, serrated edges (handle with care!), but they tend to lose their lustre as the year progresses and should be cut off altogether in autumn so that the flowers can be shown off to their best. Hellebores grow to a height and spread of no more than 18in but they do self-seed freely. These seedlings are easily trans-planted and within a year you can expect your first flowers, although they will not necessarily be the same as those on the parent plant.

Despite its Latin name, the Christmas rose, *Helleborus niger*, has pure white flowers. These stand out proudly next to the dark-green leaves, but if you are looking for a wider range of colours, try varie-ties of *Helleborus hybridus*. Named varieties of this species – espe-cially the doubles – are not cheap (sometimes £12 or more from nurseries), but many mass-market online garden retailers offer half a dozen unnamed varieties in assorted colours for roughly the same price. This represents much better value, especially as – once established – your hellebores should live for years and add a little brightness to those gloomy winter months.

Likes Partial shade, moist soil.
Flowering season December–April.
Key points Valuable winter colour, beautiful patterned flowers, long flowering period, long-lived plants. Happy on heavy soil, self-seeds freely.
VFM 10

Hemerocallis (Daylily)

From its common name you might think that the hemerocallis would be temperamental and difficult to grow. Not a bit of it. Daylilies will prosper in any soil (including heavy clay), really only need watering during times of drought, are extremely hardy and come in a huge range of colours and patterns. Look online and you will find singles and doubles, selfs (flowers of a single colour), stripes, and flowers with spectacular contrasting eyes in every colour from white to black (with the exception of a true blue). Daylilies vary in height from 18in to 3ft or more, and, according to the variety, individual flowers can be anything from 2in in diameter to a whopping 7in. Some varieties are also fragrant.

They do prefer a sunny spot (apart from the dark-red or black varieties which need some afternoon shade to prevent their colour fading), and beware of planting the crowns too deep: 1in below the surface of the soil is the recommended depth. If planted too deep, they will produce plenty of leaves but not many flowers. Ideally give them an open position where they are not hemmed in by other, bigger, plants. Even if you follow these rules, you may still find that your daylily fails to bloom in its first year. Be patient: the second year's blooms will be worth waiting for. As its name suggests, each daylily flower opens for just a single day, but the buds are carried on the sturdy stems (known as scapes) in such profusion that the display from each plant can last for several weeks. If possible, remove the dead blooms on a daily basis. This not only keeps the plant looking neat and tidy but also gives the emerging buds more room to open.

There is only one real pest: the hemerocallis gall midge, a persistent blighter that destroys some of the buds once it takes a foothold in the garden. Daylily buds should be long and slender, but those attacked by the gall midge will be shorter and fatter, and sometimes dry and wrinkled. If you see signs of infestation, pinch off the bud at the earliest opportunity and put it in a sealed plastic bag to kill the larvae inside. Don't simply throw the bud on the compost heap; doing so will allow the midge to continue its life cycle. The good news is that the midge only tends to affect the early-season varieties, so if you focus largely on plants that bloom from the end of June onwards, you shouldn't have too many problems. Even with the early-summer varieties, the midge usually only damages a few buds, and since each plant can carry dozens of buds at a time, the end result is rarely catastrophic. In any case, it does not affect the overall health of the plant – it just means that your floral display will be reduced that year. Otherwise, plant care amounts to nothing more than cutting back the stems after flowering (this may occasionally induce a second flush) and tidying up the dead strap-like leaves in the autumn. In fact, your biggest problem with daylilies will be which varieties to choose as there are hundreds available. Here are a few of the best:

'**Chicago Apache**' has rich, velvety scarlet blooms with a yellow throat. The flowers are 5in in diameter and often produce a second flush. Height and spread 2ft 3in. Late season (June–Aug).

'**Daring Deception**' has sumptuous lavender-pink outer petals with a purple picotee edge and a large, deep-purple eye (picotee flowers have petals whose edge is a contrasting – usually a darker – colour). The individual flowers are 5in across and it often reblooms. Height and spread 2ft. Mid-season (June–July).

'**Double Dream**' has neat double coral-apricot flowers that measure just over 4in across. Height and spread 2ft. Early season (May–June).

'**Double River Wye**' has exquisite double pale-yellow flowers that measure a little over 4in across. Height 4ft, spread 3ft. Mid-season (June–July).

'**El Desperado**' has crimped bright-yellow flowers with a contrasting burgundy picotee edge, a burgundy eye and a yellow-green throat. Each flower can last 16 hours and measure 5in across. Height and spread 3ft. Late season (July–Aug).

'Fulva Flore Pleno' (aka **'Kwanso'**) has magnificent double orange blooms with red markings. Each flower measures 5in across and they are produced over a long period. Height 4ft, spread 3ft. Mid-season (June–Aug).

'Indian Paintbrush' has stunning orange blooms with a red eye and a golden throat. Each flower has a diameter of 5in and the plant reaches a height and spread of 2ft 6in. Mid-season (June–July).

'Lake Effect' has large mauve flowers with a grey eye and a lime-green throat, each bloom measuring 5in across. Height and spread 2ft. Mid-season (June–July).

'Mini Pearl' produces an abundance of soft peach-coloured flowers over a long period on a compact plant that reaches a height and spread of only 18in. Each flower measures more than 3in across. Early to mid-season (May–July).

'Moussaka' has stunning large cream flowers with a purple picotee edge, a huge purple eye and a yellow throat. Each flower measures 5in across. Height and spread 2ft. Mid-season (June–July).

'Planet Max' is a spider daylily, the name given to types that have longer, thinner petals than the standard form. The length of the petal will often be at least four times its width. 'Planet Max' has open purple blooms with a contrasting lemon-yellow throat, and each flower measures 7in across. It grows up to 3ft 6in tall with a 3ft spread. Mid-season (June–July).

'Scentual Sundance' is a fragrant, long-flowering, deep-yellow self with 5in blooms. Height and spread 2ft 6in. Late season (July–Aug).

'Snowy Apparition' has fragrant white flowers with a creamy-green throat, each bloom measuring over 6in across. Height and spread 2ft 6in. Mid-season (June–July).

'Tangerine Tango' produces 4in-wide, ruffled tangerine flowers with a lime throat on a compact plant. Height and spread 18in. Mid-season (June–July).

'Voodoo Dancer' has fragrant, double, dark-purple-black flowers and a yellow throat, each bloom measuring over 5in across. They are produced on a plant that reaches a height and spread of 2ft. **Mid- to late season (June–Aug).**

'Wild Horses' is a dazzling spider daylily with cream outer petals, a giant purple eye and a yellow throat. Each bloom is 7in across. Height and spread 3ft. **Mid-season (June–July).**

Likes Any soil; most varieties need a sunny spot.

Flowering season June–August (depending on variety).

Key points Vast range of colours, likes any soil, needs little attention, will last for years.

VFM 9

Heuchera 'Obsidian'

Although they have dainty pink or white flowers, these days heucheras are primarily grown for their dazzling foliage. Whereas once upon a time they were unremarkable garden perennials with plain green leaves, their popularity has been boosted enormously by the introduction of new varieties that form neat mounds of leaves in fluorescent lime green, fiery orange, caramel and burnt copper. Look in any plant catalogue and you will struggle not to fall in love with *H.* **'Peach Flambe'** (peachy-plum leaves), *H.* **'Lime Rickey'** (lime-green leaves) or *H.* **'Marmalade'** (honey and amber leaves). These and other similarly coloured varieties are indeed beautiful plants, and with a height and spread of no more than 18in it is easy to be persuaded that there is room for a few of them in your garden.

But they can be tricky. They need good drainage, a location with some shade, and the crown of the plant has a tendency to push itself out of the ground after a few years, necessitating lifting and replanting. Without attention, the compact dome that looked so attractive in the catalogue and when the plant was young can soon develop into an ungainly mess. Fortunately not all of the new coloured-leaved heucheras are so temperamental. The varieties with dark maroon, almost black, leaves will tolerate more by way of sun, and *H.* **'Obsidian'** has flourished in my garden for years in full sun, in a spot that occasionally becomes waterlogged in winter, and without ever needing to be lifted. It has also retained its original compact shape.

When planting, the crown should be just above the surface of the soil, but once it is in place it seems happy left to its own devices, although it will benefit from a spring mulch. Any leaves that die off should be removed to keep the plant looking neat. The sultry dark foliage remains evergreen in mild winters, giving year-round interest, but even if the leaves do succumb to sharp frosts the plant itself bounces back the following spring. The new leaves are a magnificent maroon, darkening as the season progresses, and the low mound is topped by 18in sprays of white flowers on dark maroon stems in mid-summer. The leaves look particularly effective next to pale-blue hardy geraniums or orange geums.

Likes Well-drained soil in sun or partial shade.
Flowering season June–July.
Key points Maroon-black leaves provide year-round interest, tougher than many other varieties.
VFM 7

Lamprocapnos formosa 'Pearl Drops' (Bleeding Heart)

The bleeding heart, *Lamprocapnos spectabilis* (formerly known as *Dicentra spectabilis*), has been a garden favourite for two hundred years, taking its name from its dark-pink, pendant, heart-shaped flowers with white tips that are borne on arching stems. It grows to a height of nearly 3ft but requires a sheltered spot as it is susceptible to damage from spring frosts in colder parts of the country.

A safer bet, therefore, is a close relation, the shorter and tougher *L. formosa* **'Pearl Drops'**, which has delicate, creamy-white heart-shaped flowers tinged with pink but only reaches a height of about 12in. This variety has the added bonus of pretty, blue-grey, fern-like foliage, from which the flowers appear in spring and remain for weeks on end, sometimes lasting until early July. It prefers a partially shaded spot but will put up with plenty of sun provided the soil retains some moisture. As such, it is well suited to growing either in a woodland planting scheme where its light flowers and foliage can brighten up a dark corner, or at the front of a herbaceous border where it can receive some shade from the taller plants behind. It will quickly spread to 3ft or more but is easy to control simply by digging up and removing any unwanted sections. You may still find this plant listed under *lamprocapnos* or *dicentra*, and to add to the confusion it is occasionally sold as **'Langtrees'** rather than **'Pearl Drops'**.

Likes Partial shade, moisture-retentive soil.
Flowering season April–July.
Key points Attractive grey leaves, long-lasting flowers.
VFM 7

Lysimachia punctata (Yellow Loosestrife)

Yellow loosestrife is one of the toughest herbaceous perennials – in fact, your biggest problem will be making sure that it doesn't take over the rest of the garden. The whorls of yellow, star-shaped flowers with darker eyes grow on 3ft stems alongside mid-green leaves, and, if left to run amok, the plant will soon spread to a width of 5ft or more. However, it is easy to keep in check by removing the outer portions and transplanting them elsewhere in the garden. It is happy in sun or partial shade, ideally where there is some moisture in the soil, so is unfazed by heavy clay. If allowed to dry out too much in baking heat, the leaves will start to wilt, but soon revive after watering.

It is a good specimen for a woodland garden or any mixed border because, while it may not be the most glamorous of border plants, it does provide a useful splash of yellow for several weeks at the height of summer. Also, because it spreads so quickly and is easy to split (and because quality plant growers consider it to be something of a thug), it is relatively inexpensive and can often be bought cheaply on market stalls. Borders sometimes need solid, reliable 'workhorse plants' that offset their more flamboyant but temperamental neighbours. Yellow loosestrife is very much the 'Nobby Stiles' of the herbaceous border.

Likes Sun or partial shade, moist soil.
Flowering season June–August.
Key points Spreads rapidly, masses of yellow flowers, easy to divide. Excellent in heavy clay, virtually indestructible.
VFM 8

Lythrum (Purple Loosestrife)

The purple loosestrife is far less invasive than its yellow cousin, its narrow spikes of starry, pink flowers rising to a height of up to 6ft but spreading no more than 18in. This makes it an ideal subject for the back of a border, where its long stems sway elegantly in the breeze for weeks on end through late summer and into autumn. It grows naturally in boggy areas, and therefore it follows that it likes moisture-retentive soil, although it does not mind whether this is in full sun or partial shade. It will thrive in heavy clay, especially if you remember to add some rotted organic matter when planting. The plant will also benefit from a mulch of leaf mould or garden compost spread around its base in spring to help retain moisture during dry spells.

As with most tough herbaceous perennials, the stems should be cut back to the ground in autumn after flowering. Otherwise, it needs no attention and will flourish in the same spot for years without the need for division. *L. virgatum* **'Dropmore Purple'** has 6ft stems packed with purple-pink flowers and narrow, dark-green leaves and a flowering season that extends for three months, July–Oct. For a shorter variety try *L. salicaria* **'Robin'**, which has magenta-pink flowers on 3ft stems (July–Sept), or *L. salicaria* **'Blush'**, which carries paler pink flowers on 3ft stems, July–Sept.

Likes Sun or partial shade, moist soil.
Flowering season July–October.
Key points Long-lasting flowers, happy in heavy clay, attracts bees and butterflies.
VFM 8

Persicaria

Some species of persicaria are nothing more than weeds, but there are also a few that work well in herbaceous borders or in a bog garden, producing tall pokers of red or pink flowers over a long period. Even these can become invasive, however, quickly spreading to cover 4ft or more, so they will need to be kept in check. They will thrive in sun or partial shade and prefer moisture-retentive soil, but if you are unable to provide this, remember to water regularly during dry periods.

The green leaves are sometimes tinted with red for added interest and the flowers readily attract bees, hoverflies and other insects. Among the most rewarding varieties are *P. amplexicaulis* **'Firetail'**, which has 4ft spikes of small crimson-red flowers that keep their colour into autumn, and *P. amplexicaulis* **'Rubie's Pink'**, which is similar but with rosy-pink flowers. *P. affinis* **'Superba'** is a shorter, 1ft-tall plant with pale-pink flowers that age to crimson above a dense mat of green leaves which turn russet-brown in autumn.

Likes Sun or partial shade, moist soil.
Flowering season July–October
Key points Long flowering period, fast growing, attracts insects.
VFM 7

Polemonium reptans (Creeping Jacob's Ladder)

Some species of Jacob's ladder – particularly the familiar blue, cottage-garden favourite *Polemonium caeruleum* – have a reputation for being short-lived perennials. The spreading *Polemonium reptans*, however, bucks the trend and, moreover, blooms for months on end. One of the finest varieties is *P. reptans* **'Lambrook Mauve'**, which throws up numerous clusters of small, lilac-mauve flowers with a yellow throat from late spring through to autumn without so much as a pause for breath, especially if you remember to deadhead regularly. The pretty, semi-bell-shaped flowers are borne on 18in-tall stems above a neat, dense clump of finely cut green foliage that spreads to cover around 18in, making it an excellent groundcover plant for the front of a border.

It thrives in either full sun or partial shade, remains virtually evergreen in mild winters, and is happy in any soil provided the drainage is adequate. To ensure this, if you garden on heavy clay, add some horticultural grit at planting time. Your reward will be months of flower in a lovely colour not widely available in garden plants. Other notable varieties of *P. reptans* include **'Stairway to Heaven'** (sky-blue flowers and pretty variegated leaves of pink, cream and green), **'Blue Pearl'** (blue flowers) and **'White Pearl'** (white).

Likes Adequate drainage in sun or partial shade.
Flowering season April–October.
Key points Very long flowering season, good groundcover plant.
VFM 8

Polygonatum hybridum (Solomon's Seal)

Polygonatum hybridum is a shade-loving plant that will thrive in a cool, woodland setting. If you have such an area in your garden, this plant is worth growing because its graceful, arching stems of oval leaves with waxy blue undersides are followed in early summer by rows of small, green-tipped, white, bell-shaped flowers, and when the flowers have finished, berry-like red or black fruits appear. So you get three points of interest for the price of one. The flowering stems are also much prized by flower arrangers.

It can reach a height of 4ft and a spread of 3ft, particularly if well-rotted compost is added at planting time and a generous, moisture-retaining mulch is applied in spring. It will grow happily in partial shade – perhaps in a mixed shrub and herbaceous border – so long as its roots are shaded from the heat of the afternoon sun. If in any doubt, water in dry weather. Cut down the stems in autumn to rejuvenate the plant for the following year.

Likes Partial to full shade, moist soil.

Flowering season May–June.

Key points Attractive foliage, white flowers and dark berries prolong the season of interest. Good for flower arrangements.

VFM 8

Potentilla (Cinquefoil)

The potentilla genus is a useful one for the gardener as it contains easy-to-grow shrubs, rockery plants and herbaceous perennials in a range of cheerful colours. The shrub and rockery cinquefoils are dealt with later in this book (see Alpines and Rockery Perennials), but there are plenty of varieties that will bring a splash of colour to the front of a border in summer. All are sun worshippers and like reasonably drained soil that does not become waterlogged in winter.

The central clump of green, strawberry-like leaves remains neat, but the flowers are produced on sprawling stems that can extend more than 2ft in all directions. This has a tendency to make the plant look untidy if grown in isolation, so if possible set it among other specimens that will help support these awkward stems while leaving the pretty potentilla flowers visible. The flowering season can often be prolonged by cutting the stems right back in late summer to encourage a second flush. Otherwise they need little attention, but if the clumps do become overcrowded, they can be lifted and divided in autumn or spring. The single varieties have saucer-shaped flowers, but some of these can be comparatively small for the size of the plant, so you may prefer to hunt out the showier doubles. Here are some of the most popular varieties (singles and doubles):

P. **'Arc-en-Ciel'** has 2in, double, dark-red flowers with yellow edges, the flowers becoming increasingly yellow as they age. June–Sept.

P. **'Flamenco'** has eye-catching, single, scarlet flowers with darker eyes over green foliage. June–Aug.

P. **'Gibson's Scarlet'** produces a mass of smallish, 1in-wide, single red flowers with a darker eye. June–Aug.

P. nepalensis **'Miss Willmott'** produces an abundance of single pink flowers with contrasting raspberry-red eyes. June–Aug.

P. recta **'Sulphurea'** is a more upright species, reaching a height of 2ft and a spread of 18in and producing single, sulphur-yellow flowers. June–Aug.

P. thurberi **'Monarch's Velvet'** has distinctive, single strawberry-red flowers with a darker eye. June–Sept.

P. **'Volcan'** produces 2in-wide, double flowers in a velvety burgundy shade that becomes even darker with age. June–Sept.

P. **'William Rollisson'** is an outstanding double with large, 2in-wide flowers that resemble oranges and lemons, each bloom being bright orange with a yellow eye and blotches. June–Sept.

Likes Decent drainage and full sun.
Flowering season June–September.
Key points Bright, cheerful flowers, single and double, over a long period. Low maintenance.
VFM 8

Primula (Primrose)

The primula genus is one of the largest of all garden plants, but while most species of primrose are short-lived and some are downright demanding, there are a few which will carry on for several years and are easy to care for. The basic requirement for almost every type of readily available primula (with the exception of *P. auricula*, which is dealt with later under Alpines and Rockery Perennials) is plenty of moisture and goodness in the soil. They are notoriously hungry plants, so when planting add rotted compost or leaf mould to the hole and mulch every spring. To achieve the moist soil they need, they prefer a partially shaded position but will grow in full sun provided you water them thoroughly as soon as the leaves start to wilt in heat.

P. denticulata, the drumstick primrose, is probably the easiest perennial primula to grow. Large pompoms composed of dozens of tiny flowers in pink-purple, pink or white rise 18in above the large, tongue-shaped leaves in spring. The darker colours look particularly effective when planted among daffodils. The clump will eventually spread to about 18in, and when it gets too big for its space, it can be lifted in late spring immediately after flowering and divided. Simply pull away any outer sections with their roots and use them as new plants. If the central section of the main plant is still healthy, replant it; if not, discard it. Either way, you should now have three or four small plants from the one parent. **April–May.**

P. japonica, the candelabra primrose, has similar requirements to *P. denticulata*, but the flowers are later and more vibrant. Instead of pompoms, they are arranged in tiers on the stout, upright stems. *P. japonica* **'Miller's Crimson'** has cerise-pink flowers with a darker eye, and *P. japonica* **'Apple Blossom'** has pale-pink flowers with a honey-coloured eye. **May–July.** The 2ft-high *P. bulleyana* is another form of candelabra primrose, but with yellow flowers, tinged with orange, that open from striking orange-crimson buds. **May–June.**

P. vulgaris, the common primrose, is one of the most fondly loved of all native plants with its large, pale-lemon flowers and darker yellow eye lighting up many a woodland in late winter and early spring. A compact plant, it only grows a few inches up and out, but self-seeds vigorously, so that although the parent plant may be relatively short-lived, its place will be taken by half a dozen or more seedlings which can be allowed to naturalise as they would in the wild. Feb–May.

Likes Partial shade, moist, rich soil.
Flowering season February–July (according to species).
Key points Lovely spring flowers, will self-seed or divide easily to make more plants.
VFM 8

Prunella grandiflora (Large Self-Heal)

While the common form of self-heal, *Prunella vulgaris*, is a herb/weed with insignificant flowers that has a tendency to appear uninvited on lawns, there is a form of prunella that is worth growing in the garden. As its name implies, *Prunella grandiflora* has larger flowers and is a useful weed-suppressing plant for the front of a border. It throws up numerous erect spikes of pink, mauve, violet, blue or white hooded flowers above a mat of semi-evergreen leaves from mid-summer onwards, sometimes blooming right the way through to autumn. Prunella takes its popular name of self-heal from its foliage, which was used to stem bleeding in medieval times. Although it might not be a true showstopper, it is a plant that does a solid job without fuss and freely attracts bees and butterflies to the garden.

Varieties of *P. grandiflora* to look out for include **'Alba'** (white), **'Bella Blue'** (violet-blue), **'Freelander Blue'** (deep violet-blue), **'Loveliness'** (lilac-blue), **'Rosea'** (rose pink) and **'Rubra'** (deep pink). These will reach a height of 9in and a spread of 18in or more and will grow in any reasonable soil in either sun or part shade. It often self-seeds and requires little attention apart from the usual deadheading and cutting the stems down to ground level in autumn. However, it will benefit from a spring mulch and might need watering in hot, dry weather. As it likes soil that does not dry out, try growing it beneath taller herbaceous plants or shrubs where it will receive a spot of dappled shade.

Likes Any reasonable, moisture-retentive soil in sun or light shade.
Flowering season June–September.
Key points Good groundcover plant with a long flowering period, attracts bees and insects. Easy to grow and keep, self-seeds.
VFM 7

Pulmonaria (Lungwort)

Pulmonaria officinalis has been grown in gardens for centuries, chiefly as a cure for respiratory diseases, hence its common name. If you have a shady or semi-shaded spot where the soil does not dry out too much in summer, the low-growing pulmonaria with its delicate flowers of white, pink or blue (and sometimes both) and its hairy, spotted leaves perfectly complements daffodils and hellebores in spring. It provides useful groundcover under trees or shrubs and needs little attention other than watering in dry weather and picking off any dead leaves in late summer.

It will benefit from the addition of rotted compost at planting time and a spring mulch to retain moisture, and will reach a height of about 10in and a spread of over 2ft in favourable conditions. The flowers are also a valuable source of nectar for newly emerging bees. These are some of the most reliable varieties:

P. **'Blue Ensign'** has vivid, gentian-blue flowers that are set against plain, dark-green leaves. Looks outstanding next to primroses and dwarf narcissi. **Feb–April.**

P. **'Diana Clare'** has flowers that open mauve-pink before ageing to cobalt blue, plus attractive silver leaves, mottled with green. **March–May.**

P. **'Opal'** has unusual ice-blue flowers and green and silver-spotted leaves. **Feb–April.**

P. rubra has interesting coral-red flowers and plain, light-green foliage. **Feb–May.**

P. saccharata **'Mrs Moon'** forms a neat mound of pink flowers fading to a soft blue, and mid-green leaves splattered with white blotches. **March–May.**

P. **'Sissinghurst White'** is a classic white variety with white-spotted, mid-green leaves. **Feb–April.**

Likes Shade, moist soil.

Flowering season February–May.

Key points Some varieties have two-tone flowers and attractive, spotted leaves. Good spring colour and valued by bees.

VFM 8

Rudbeckia fulgida var. sullivantii 'Goldsturm' (Coneflower)

The rudbeckia genus is a fine source of autumn colour in the garden, where their yellows, oranges and bronzes complement blue or purple Michaelmas daisies. Although sometimes sold as perennials, most of the orange, dark-red and bronze rudbeckias are best grown as annuals. Of the true perennials, the 3ft-high *R. gloriosa* **'Goldquelle'** has sunny, double, yellow flowers but also has an unfortunate tendency to be eaten by slugs and so may be best avoided.

However, there are no such problems with *R. fulgida* **'Goldsturm'**, which is one of the toughest, most dependable and longest flowering of all herbaceous perennials. Its single, yellow, daisy-like flowers with contrasting blackish-brown cone centres first open in July and bloom profusely non-stop until the end of October, sometimes even into November. As they age, the petals acquire an attractive amber tint. It only grows to just over 2ft high on sturdy stems, so it needs no staking or support and will after a couple of years fill out an area more than 3ft square. If the outer sections become too invasive for your space, you can simply dig them up and plant them elsewhere. One parent plant can give a dozen or more smaller individual specimens, and you don't have to go to the trouble of lifting and dividing the whole plant or taking cuttings. It is propagation made easy.

Over the years, as with other herbaceous perennials such as asters, the centre of the plant will begin to look tired, so dig up the centre in spring, throw it away and replace it with some sections from the outside of the plant. Instant repairs! The only other consideration is to make sure it has enough water on hot summer days. Although it prefers to be planted in a sunny spot, its leaves can wilt in extreme heat, but a good soaking from a watering can or hose will quickly revive it.

Likes Reasonably drained soil in sun or light shade.

Flowering season July–October.

Key points Long flowering season, easy to divide, will flourish for years.

VFM 10

Saponaria officinalis (Soapwort)

When tapestries needed cleaning in medieval times, the leaves of *Saponaria officinalis* were rubbed together to form a lather – and that gave the plant its common name. Instead of washrooms, it is now more commonly found in herbaceous borders where its fragrant, double pink or white flowers borne on 2ft-tall stems in late summer and early autumn have made it a cottage-garden favourite. The native wild flower form, which has single pink blooms, is too invasive for most gardens and has now largely been replaced by the double-flowering varieties, *S. officinalis* **'Rubra Plena'** (cerise), **'Rosea Plena'** (pale pink) and **'Alba Plena'** (white). Not that these are exactly shy, capable of spreading up to 3ft. Nor are they fussy, thriving even in poor, dry soil and in either full sun or light shade. In fact, if the soil is too rich, the stems have a tendency to flop and may require some support. Otherwise, they need little attention. Just cut down the stems in autumn to promote fresh growth the following year.

Likes Any soil in sun or light shade.
Flowering season July–September.
Key points Easy to grow, fragrant flowers, drought tolerant.
VFM 7

Saxifraga urbium (London Pride)

Most saxifrages are best suited to the rock garden where their need for soil with excellent drainage keeps them out of the 'easy to grow' category. However, the larger *Saxifraga urbium* is considerably less fussy and makes a good subject for the front of a shady border that retains some moisture. It is an old staple of cottage gardens, popularly known as 'London Pride' or the enchanting 'Look Up and Kiss Me' as well as the less flattering 'St Patrick's Cabbage'.

It is fair to say that it is a plant that divides opinion among gardeners. It could never be described as the most spectacular of perennials, but it is worth growing for its easy-going nature and its low mat of evergreen rosettes above which rise delicate, pale-pink starry flowers on 1ft-high, slender red stems. It will spread quite rapidly to about 18in but is easily kept in check. For something a little more exotic, try *S. urbium* **'Aureopunctata'**, which has attractive variegated leaves.

Likes Any soil in partial shade.
Flowering season May–July.
Key points Dainty pink flowers, evergreen foliage.
VFM 6

Thalictrum delavayi 'Hewitt's Double' (Meadow Rue)

This tall, upright, clump-forming, rhizomatous perennial is ideal for planting at the back of a border next to a hedge or a fence, where its slender stems can be supported naturally on all sides and where it will not be buffeted by strong winds. If set in a more open location, the stems will need staking, which can spoil the overall look of the plant. It produces light, airy sprays of small, lilac-mauve, pompom flowers that are similar in shape to those of gypsophila. For added interest, the stems are flushed dark purple (especially in full sun) and the dainty, mid-green leaves resemble those of maidenhair fern. A mature plant will remain in bloom for several weeks in late summer, extending into early autumn if the weather is favourable.

It will grow in sun or dappled shade and, despite its delicate appearance, is completely hardy. It is unfussy about soil, provided there is some moisture all year round, so add rotted compost at planting time and mulch in spring. Cut the stems down to ground level in late autumn. Clumps can be divided every few years in spring to maintain the plant's vigour, although it is worth noting that the divided sections may take a while to re-establish. It will eventually reach a height of 4ft and a spread of 2ft. There is also a white form of *T. delavayi* – **'Album'** – that has single flowers with yellow stamens. This prefers a partially highlighted site and grows to a height of 5ft with a spread of almost 3ft. **July–Oct.**

Likes Sun or light shade, moist soil.
Flowering season July–October.
Key points Long-lasting mauve flowers, attractive purple stems. Flowers and dainty foliage are used in flower arranging.
VFM 7

Tradescantia andersoniana (Spiderwort)

On the face of it, the hardy tradescantia should be more widely grown than it is. After all, it is happy in any soil (even surviving in ground that becomes temporarily waterlogged in winter), thrives in both sun or partial shade and has large, open, three-petalled flowers in colours not readily found in garden plants, including a true purple (as opposed to some of the dark pinks that call themselves purple) and the iciest of ice blues. The buds are produced in such profusion that there is a continuous succession of flowers for up to three months, and there are also varieties with attractive, golden leaves. So why isn't it more popular?

The answer, I suspect, is because the stems that carry the buds and the sword-shaped leaves on taller varieties tend to flop, so even though the plant doesn't grow much over 18in in height, it needs support – a requirement that doesn't really lend itself to a position at the front of a border. If you are unable to provide sufficient support to stop the plant looking untidy, simply cut it back to the ground as soon as it collapses. This will rejuvenate the plant and quickly produce a fresh flush of flowers. *T. andersoniana* will eventually spread to 2ft. If the clumps become too large, they can be divided in autumn or spring. Here are some of the prettiest varieties:

T. andersoniana **'Blue and Gold'** (aka **'Sweet Kate'**) has lovely yellow, grassy foliage that perfectly complements its rich blue flowers. This only reaches a height of 1ft, so is less prone to flopping.

T. andersoniana **'Blue Stone'** has large, lavender-blue flowers with pale-yellow stamens and mid-green leaves.

T. andersoniana **'Concord Grape'** has purple-tinged green leaves offset by large purple flowers with bright yellow stamens.

T. andersoniana **'Osprey'** has mid-green leaves topped by white flowers with subtle blue flushing and a blue centre, creating an overall effect of ice blue.

T. andersoniana **'Red Grape'** has dark grey-green leaves and clusters of mauve-pink flowers with contrasting yellow stamens.

Likes Any soil in sun or partial shade.

Flowering season June–September.

Key points Grows in any soil and in any location except deep shade. Long flowering period.

VFM 7

Trollius cultorum (Globe Flower)

It is not always easy to find perennials that will flourish in boggy ground, but the globe flower is one that certainly does. Good drainage is not an issue with this plant; in fact, it must have moist soil, making it an excellent specimen for growing alongside a pond or on heavy clay that does not dry out. To ensure that sufficient moisture is retained through summer, add plenty of rotted compost at planting time, give it a mulch in spring and water in hot weather. In return, you can expect a late-spring show of large, bowl-shaped flowers – as big as 2in across – in shades of yellow on sturdy 2ft stems above a clump of neat green leaves. If you cut back the stems immediately after flowering, you may be rewarded with a second crop of blooms.

In the right conditions this is a plant that will thrive for many years without needing much by way of care. Among the best cultivars are **'Alabaster'** (soft cream), **'Lemon Queen'** (pale yellow), **'Orange Princess'** (orange-gold) and **'Superbus'** (golden yellow).

Likes Moist soil in sun or partial shade.

Flowering season May–June.

Key points Large, globular flowers, good for a pondside location. Long-lived.

VFM 7

PART II

Alpines and rockery perennials

Alpine plants require excellent drainage – and usually a sunny spot – to replicate the mountain conditions where they grow in the wild. Without this, some of the choicest alpines will rot in wet British winters but there are a few more accommodating species, along with a selection of dwarf perennials that are suitable for growing in a rockery, and these are the plants I have listed here. Even so, always add a good quantity of horticultural grit both in the planting hole and as a collar around the base of the plant. This gritty mulch should be replenished every couple of years when the original layer has been washed away. Given the conditions they desire, these plants will live for years and, because rockery plants are considerably cheaper than herbaceous perennials, they offer excellent value for money.

Arabis

Arabis is an easy-to-grow perennial forming sizeable clumps of lightly fragrant, white or pink flowers that look their best when tumbling down banks and rockeries in spring. It will grow in poor soils and, once established, is drought tolerant. Allowed to run wild, most varieties of *A. alpina* will take over a small rockery (the evergreen foliage soon covering 2ft or more), but can be restrained by cutting back the straggly stems after flowering. It reaches a height of around 9in, and although it prefers full sun, it will put up with some light shade.

A. alpina subsp. caucasica **'Snowcap'** produces masses of white flowers, and there is also a double form, *A. alpina subsp. caucasica* **'Flore Pleno'**, which has larger white flowers, although not in such great numbers. Meanwhile *A. alpina subsp. caucasica* **'Variegata'** carries single, white flowers above attractive green and cream variegated leaves. *A. alpina subsp. caucasica* **'Little Treasure Deep Rose'** is a more compact variety, spreading to just over 1ft and producing rosy-pink flowers for weeks in spring. If you can find it, try *A. blepharophylla* **'Red Sensation'**, which has small purple-pink flowers. It reaches a height of 4in and a spread of little more than 1ft, making it more manageable if space is in short supply.

Likes Sun or light shade, well-drained soil.

Flowering season March–May.

Key points Reliable splash of spring colour, easy to grow, prospers in poor soils, drought tolerant. Flowers are lightly fragrant.

VFM 8

Armeria (Thrift)

With its dense clusters of neat, rounded pink flowers produced from hummocks of grassy leaves, thrift (sea pink) is a familiar sight growing in rocky crevices and on clifftops in coastal regions of Britain. Therefore the aim of the gardener wishing to grow this tough little evergreen perennial should be to replicate its natural habitat. Give it good drainage and a dry, sunny spot and squeeze it between rocks. You can even plant it horizontally between two rocks (which will further improve winter drainage), but make sure the planting hole is filled with gritty soil (it prefers poor soil).

Thrift reaches a height of 8in and a spread of less than 1ft, making it a good, compact plant for any rockery, especially if you have a windy, coastal plot where less robust plants struggle. It also works well in a gravel garden, particularly on an open, exposed site. The native *A. maritima* is pink, but you can also buy *A. maritima* **'Alba'** (white). Deadhead immediately after flowering to encourage a second flush. All varieties are popular with bees and butterflies.

Likes Full sun, well-drained soil.
Flowering season May–July.
Key points Neat hummocks of pink or white flowers. Happy in poor soil, drought tolerant, tough, attracts bees and butterflies.
VFM 8

Aubrieta

Rockeries may no longer be quite as popular as they were thirty years ago, but even if you just have a drystone wall, no plant will look better cascading down it than the blue, mauve, red or pink of aubrieta, the country's favourite alpine. Its rich colours form the perfect backdrop for clumps of dwarf narcissi, and if cut back to about half its size immediately after flowering it will grow with renewed vigour the following year, while allowing its quieter neighbours to enjoy their moment in the spotlight.

If left unattended, aubrieta will spread to cover 2ft or more, swamping everything in its path. It also becomes straggly and untidy, so an annual late spring trim will work wonders. When carrying out this haircut, you can take any unwanted stems that have roots and plant them elsewhere in the garden – even in path crevices where there is hardly any soil. You'll be amazed at how quickly they will form a green mat. Alternatively, peg low-growing stems into the ground and cover with light soil or sand, and they will soon root. Then simply cut the rooted stem from the parent and replant. Aubrieta grows to a height of 3in, must have full sun, and thrives on light chalky soil, although it will tolerate any well-drained soil.

There are many splendid hybrids to choose from, including double and variegated forms. Among the best are *A.* **'Astolat'** (blue-mauve flowers and variegated foliage), *A.* **'Blue Beauty'** (double purple-blue flowers), *A.* **'Bressingham Red'** (dark-red flowers with compact foliage), *A.* **'Double Pink'** (double pink flowers), *A.* **'Purple Cascade'** (mauve), *A.* **'Red Cascade'** (magenta), *A.* **'Spring Cascade'** (pink) and *A.* **'Swan Red'** (purple-red).

Likes Full sun, well-drained soil.
Flowering season March–May.
Key points Masses of red or blue flowers look great with dwarf narcissi, easy to increase numbers. Ideal for drystone walls.
VFM 9

Aurinia (Alyssum)

The sight of yellow alyssum cascading down rockeries next to blue aubrieta was a favourite combination in British spring gardens for decades. And with good reason, because when in bloom the numerous heads of bright golden flowers cover the entire plant, completely obliterating the grey-green leaves. Give *Aurinia saxatilis* – the most commonly grown species – well-drained soil in a sunny spot and it will soon grow to a height of 9in and spread close to 2ft, so it makes quite a statement. It is particularly happy on poor sandy or chalk soils. The downside is that it is unsuitable for a small rockery, but you can keep it in check by cutting back the stems hard after flowering. This will not only improve the following year's display, but will also help extend the life of the plant.

In garden centres you are most likely to find the basic golden-yellow variety, but for a more subtle shade seek out *A. saxatilis* **'Citrinum'**, which has paler, lemon-yellow flowers, or *A. saxatilis* **'Variegata'** with its variegated leaves. For a more compact alyssum try *A. montanum*, which grows about 4in tall and covers no more than 1ft. You may also still find aurinia sold under its old name of alyssum.

Likes Full sun, well-drained soil.

Flowering season April–June.

Key points Combines well with aubrieta, produces hundreds of yellow flowers. Thrives on poor soils.

VFM 7

Campanula poscharskyana
(Trailing Bellflower)

Members of the campanula genus are among the most versatile of garden performers – ranging from tall border perennials to dwarf alpines – but many require light, chalky soils to be at their best, and almost all are prone to being killed off by snails. An exception to both rules is the dwarf perennial *Campanula poscharskyana*, which is less fussy about soil conditions and, while still attractive to snails, grows so quickly that the munching molluscs are simply unable to keep up with it. They may destroy the odd leaf but they will rarely be able to savage the entire plant. For whereas other species of alpine campanula, such as *C. carpatica* or *C. muralis*, grow at a leisurely pace, *C. poscharskyana* lives life in the fast lane, quickly spreading to a height of 8in and a spread of 2ft or more. In doing so, it produces masses of pretty, star-shaped, lavender-blue flowers in late summer and autumn – a time when many alpines have finished their displays.

It will prosper in either full sun or partial shade and, although well-drained soil is advisable, it does like some moisture and will grow equally well at the front of a border as on a rockery. It is arguably the toughest of all campanulas, but it can become invasive, so cut it back after flowering to maintain some semblance of shape. There are also white forms – notably *C. poscharskyana* **'E. H. Frost'** – the flowers of which contrast nicely with the mid-green leaves.

Likes Sun or partial shade, moist, well-drained soil.
Flowering season June–September.
Key points Tough, undemanding, spreads quickly, long flowering season.
VFM 8

Erigeron karvinskianus (Mexican Fleabane)

The Mexican fleabane is a tough little perennial that is useful for scrambling down rockeries or drystone walls. It bears dozens of small, white, daisy-like flowers that turn pink with age and it self-seeds freely, eventually forming a 10in-tall mat of narrow, hairy leaves covering at least 2ft of ground, which may make it too thuggish for a small rockery. It likes a sunny spot and well-drained soil and should be trimmed back after flowering to help curb its invasive tendencies. The flowers may be relatively insignificant – unless you happen to be fond of the common daisy – but it does bloom for a longer period than most rockery plants, right through summer and into early autumn. It is also handy for planting in steps and narrow crevices, where most other plants would struggle to survive.

Likes Full sun, well-drained soil.
Flowering season June–September.
Key points Tough, long flowering period, self-seeds.
VFM 7

Helianthemum nummularium (Rock Rose)

Although technically a small shrub, the helianthemum is most commonly found in gardens on sun-baked rockeries, drystone walls or at the front of raised beds where, over many weeks in summer, it produces a profusion of large, saucer-shaped flowers in colours ranging from white to deep red. Many of these colours are not available in any other easy-to-grow rockery plant, making the helianthemum an important consideration for any alpine plan.

Grown in full sun (the flowers may not even open on dull days) and soil with decent drainage, it will reach an ultimate height of 1ft and a spread of over 2ft, but it should be trimmed back after flowering, partly to keep a neat shape and also to encourage a second flush of blooms. It is either entirely or semi- evergreen, thereby providing year-round interest, and some varieties have attractive narrow grey leaves. There are also forms with double flowers. Here are some of the best rock roses:

H. **'Ben Affleck'** has large, cheerful yellow flowers with prominent orange centres and glossy green leaves.

H. **'Ben Ledi'** has glossy dark leaves and large, rose-pink flowers with darker centres and yellow eyes.

H. **'Ben Mohr'** has dark orange – almost copper-coloured – flowers with yellow centres and grey-green leaves.

H. **'Burgundy Dazzler'** has burgundy-red flowers with yellow eyes and glossy, dark-green leaves.

H. **'Cerise Queen'** produces masses of double, cerise-pink flowers with yellow centres above glossy green leaves.

H. **'Fire Dragon'** bears saucer-shaped, orange-red flowers with yellow eyes, which stand out against its grey leaves.

H. **'Henfield Brilliant'** has vivid, brick-red flowers with yellow eyes and beautiful grey leaves.

H. **'Highdown Apricot'** produces delicate, pale-apricot flowers with yellow centres above dark-green leaves.

H. **'Jubilee'** has double, primrose-yellow flowers and dark-green leaves.

H. **'Raspberry Ripple'** has dazzling flowers of dark pink and white, just like the ice cream of the same name. The foliage is glossy green.

H. **'Wisley Pink'** has pale-pink flowers with centres that are flushed with yellow against a backdrop of grey leaves.

H. **'Wisley Primrose'** produces large, primrose-yellow flowers with darker golden centres and grey leaves.

H. **'Wisley White'** has white, yellow-centred flowers held above dark green leaves.

Likes Full sun, well-drained soil.

Flowering season May–July.

Key points Wide range of colours in summer, large flowers. Forms a neat, long-lived evergreen shrub, excellent for trailing down banks.

VFM 9

Iberis sempervirens (Perennial Candytuft)

Few white garden flowers come much purer than those of the perennial candytuft, *Iberis sempervirens*. This easy-to-grow, long-lived, mat-forming evergreen produces hundreds of densely packed heads of snowy-white blooms, offset by shiny, narrow, dark-green leaves. Ideal for tumbling down rock gardens or walls, it will grow in any reasonably drained soil and will even thrive in poor ground, provided it gets plenty of sun.

It reaches a height of 1ft and a spread of 18in, and it is advisable to give it a trim after flowering to keep the plant's shape and to prevent it becoming too invasive. If space is limited, try *I. sempervirens* **'Little Gem'** (aka **'Weisser Zwerg'**) which has equally lovely white flowers but only reaches a height of 6in and a spread of 8in.

Likes Full sun, well-drained soil.

Flowering season May–June.

Key points Long-lived, easy to grow, even in poor soil. Pure white flowers, evergreen foliage.

VFM 8

Lysimachia nummularia 'Aurea'
(Golden Creeping Jenny)

Whereas most rockery plants demand well-drained soil and full sun, this dwarf lysimachia prefers moist earth and some shade. Add a little leaf mould at planting time to improve the soil and to help retain moisture during dry spells, and you will be rewarded with a golden carpet all year round. For even when the bright yellow, cup-shaped flowers are not in bloom, the golden-yellow leaves on this evergreen variety provide a delightful display. There is also the common, green-leaved *Lysimachia nummularia*, but that is too invasive for most gardens. Not that *L. nummularia* **'Aurea'** is exactly shy, growing vigorously on creeping stems to cover an area of 2ft or more. It only reaches a height of about 4in, and therefore makes an excellent groundcover plant for damp locations, such as the sides of a pond.

Likes Moist soil in sun or partial shade.
Flowering season June–July.
Key points Undemanding, creeping evergreen perennial with golden foliage all year round.
VFM 8

Ophiopogon planiscapus 'Nigrescens' (Lilyturf or Black Mondo Grass)

This dwarf perennial only reaches a height of 8in and a spread of 1ft, but what it lacks in substance it more than makes up for in style. It has eye-catching, jet-black, spidery, grass-like leaves, and as the plant is evergreen, these are borne all year round. In summer it throws up small spikes of bell-shaped, lilac-mauve flowers, which are in turn followed by glossy, blue-black berries. It will grow in full sun or partial shade and likes moist but well-drained, humus-rich soil. So at planting time, add leaf mould or rotted compost mixed in with plenty of horticultural grit. An additional collar of grit around the crown of the plant will help to protect the all-important foliage.

The black leaves and compact habit make it an excellent rock-garden specimen, especially when planted near spring bulbs or low-growing pink, orange or pale-blue perennials, such as *Potentilla tonguei* or *Veronica prostrata*. Although it is probably too small for the front of a border, it also works well when planted in a gravel garden, especially when using golden gravel. It is completely hardy and needs no special care but can be propagated by division in spring.

Likes Moist, well-drained soil in full sun or partial shade.
Flowering season June–July.
Key points Black leaves, lilac flowers, blue-black berries. Evergreen for year-round interest.
VFM 8

Potentilla (Rock Cinquefoil)

There are a number of species of potentilla that are suitable for growing on rock gardens. They produce a succession of cheerful flowers – usually yellow – over a long period and some have attractive, silvery leaves. All prefer a position in full sun and will grow in any reasonable garden soil, although the addition of a little horticultural grit at planting time will do no harm. They do not outgrow their space, are completely hardy and, for the minimum of attention, will prosper for years. These are some of the best:

P. alba has large, white flowers with yellow eyes above a mat of dark-green leaves. Height 6in, spread 8in. **April–June.**

P. crantzii, the alpine cinquefoil, produces yellow, cup-shaped flowers with apricot markings on longish stems. Height 8in, spread 1ft. **March–May**.

P. megalantha has large yellow flowers set among pretty grey-green foliage. Height and spread 9in. **June–Aug.**

P. neumanniana **'Nana'**, the spring cinquefoil, produces masses of golden-yellow buttercup flowers above pretty green leaves in spring and early summer, and often again in the autumn. Height 3in, spread 1ft. **April–June.**

P. tonguei is a stunning little cinquefoil bearing good-sized flowers of peachy apricot with a darker red eye – an unusual colour for the garden. These are borne on long stems from a compact mound of handsome green leaves. Height 6in, spread 18in. **June–Aug.**

Likes Full sun.

Flowering season Varies according to species.

Key points Long-lived, long flowering season. Requires little attention, unfussy about soil conditions.

VFM 9

Primula auricula

Every spring, garden shops and supermarkets are full of trays of magnificent polyanthus plants bearing huge flowers in a vast array of shades from white to navy blue. It is hard not to be seduced by these beauties, and indeed they are invaluable for injecting a vibrant splash of container-based colour into your patch. When they have finished flowering, you can then plant them out in the garden in the hope that they will repeat the performance the following spring. The reality, however – even if you remember to give them a good mulch – is that, within a year or two, they will have vanished. While technically they are perennials, they are short-lived perennials.

However, another member of the primula genus, the auricula, is a true perennial and, given the right conditions, will thrive in your garden for years. Avoid show auriculas – they are too temperamental – and concentrate instead on border or garden auriculas, which are tougher and less demanding. They grow naturally in alpine regions, making them extremely hardy and ideal for rockeries, but they hate poor drainage and too much hot summer sun. So add plenty of horticultural grit when planting – both in the hole and around the collar of the plant – and put them in a position where they receive some dappled shade from the midday sun. Do not be tempted to plant them in full shade, however.

Auriculas have pale green, fleshy leaves, above which rise large, single flowers in maroon, purple, lilac, brick-red, blue or yellow, most with a unique, dual-coloured outer ring and all with big, contrasting white or pale-yellow eyes. Study them at close quarters and you will see that few small garden plants can match the sheer beauty of their flowers – no wonder enthusiasts have exhibited them for centuries. The stems are about 9in long and each carries a number of buds. In time, the plant will spread to 1ft. Double auriculas are also available – in interesting colours such as ginger and navy blue – but, to me, these lack the subtlety of shade of the singles, and the flowers can be disappointingly small. You can obtain named auricula varieties individually from specialist suppliers, but a more economic method is to buy a dozen or so mixed-border auriculas from a mass-market garden retailer. These will work out at well under £1 per plant and should give you years of pleasure. Although their official flowering time is spring, they will sometimes produce a second, lesser, crop of flowers as late as October. The only mystery with auriculas is why they are not more popular with gardeners today.

Likes Well-drained soil in light shade.

Flowering season March–May.

Key points Fabulous flowers like miniature artworks, tough, hardy, last for years.

VFM 9

Pulsatilla vulgaris (Pasque Flower)

Rarely found in the wild in the UK, the pasque flower is one of the prettiest of all rock-garden plants, its silky, finely dissected leaves topped with large, 3in-wide, golden-centred, bell-shaped flowers in violet-purple or maroon, which are carried on 4in upright stems. It remains compact, the clump spreading to no more than 8in. Its dark flowers combine well with dwarf spring narcissi, although a white variety (*P. vulgaris* **'Alba'**) is also available. As it takes up so little space, you could try planting it in a rockery in a group of three. When it has finished blooming do not be tempted to deadhead because the plant goes on to form attractive silvery seed-heads that prolong the period of interest. The pasque flower should be planted firmly in well-drained soil in a sunny spot and resents disturbance, so do not try to move it.

Likes Full sun, well-drained soil.
Flowering season April–May.
Key points Beautiful dark flowers, silky leaves and seed-heads.
VFM 8

Sedum (Stonecrop)

The sedum genus contains a number of species suitable for growing in the crevices of a rock garden. A few, such as the yellow-flowered *S. acre* and its white cousin *S. album*, will quickly form a low mat covering 3ft or more. Although these are fine for trailing down a drystone wall or a bank, they are too invasive for a small rockery. However, there are plenty of more compact forms – many with attractive foliage – which are easy to grow provided you give them plenty of sun and well-drained soil. These are some of the best:

S. kamtschaticum **'Variegatum'** has small, star-shaped orange-yellow flowers which age to crimson. These are produced above a mat of pretty, fleshy, green leaves with pink tints and cream edges that give year-round interest. Will tolerate light shade. Height 4in, spread 10in. June–July.

S. **'Ruby Glow'** bears large, flat heads of star-shaped, ruby-red flowers above clumps of fleshy, purple-green leaves. The nectar-rich flowers of this variety are particularly attractive to butterflies and bees and it will tolerate some shade. Height 10in, spread 18in. July–Sept.

S. rupestre **'Chocolate Ball'** has chocolate-brown, semi-evergreen leaves which contrast with its orange-yellow flowers. Will tolerate light shade. Height 3in, spread 18in. July–Sept.

S. spathulifolium **'Cape Blanco'** has thick, purple-tinged, grey-green leaves and small clusters of starry, yellow flowers. As it is ever-green, the foliage is excellent for providing winter interest. Attracts butterflies and bees and tolerates light shade. Height 4in, spread 2ft. June–July. *S. spathulifolium* **'Purpureum'** is grown mainly for its outstanding succulent, purple-leaved rosettes, the inner sections of which are a contrasting silver. It forms clusters of small, star-shaped flowers over a long period. Attracts butterflies and bees and is happy in sun or light shade. Height 4in, spread 2ft. June–Aug.

S. spurium **'Album Superbum'** has white flowers and rosettes of green leaves that turn red in autumn. Happy in sun or light shade.

Height 4in, spread 1ft. June–Aug. *S. spurium* **'Coccineum'** (or **'Dragon's Blood'**) produces deep-crimson blooms above bronze-green evergreen foliage. Tolerates light shade. Height 4in, spread 1ft. June–Aug.

Likes Full sun or light shade, well-drained soil.

Flowering season Varies according to species.

Key points Colourful evergreen foliage provides year-round interest. Pretty, star-shaped flowers, attractive to butterflies and bees.

VFM 9

Silene uniflora 'Robin Whitebreast' (Sea Campion)

Also known as *S. maritima* **'Flore Pleno'**, this enchanting little semi-evergreen sea campion makes an excellent rockery plant, producing double white flowers over a long period through late summer and into autumn above a mat of grey-green leaves. The flowers are exceptionally large for a plant of this size, measuring 1.5in across, making them the size of a carnation. It needs well-drained soil but will grow in either full sun or light shade, reaching a height of 6in and a spread of 1ft.

Another easy-to-grow, semi-evergreen rock silene is *S. schafta*, which produces an abundance of dainty, five-petalled, magenta-pink flowers from late summer against a backdrop of lance-shaped green leaves. It likes the same conditions as *S. uniflora* and it, too, reaches a height of 6in and a spread of about 1ft.

Likes Well-drained soil in full sun or light shade.
Flowering season July–October.
Key points Long, late flowering season, providing rockery interest into October.
VFM 8

Thymus (Thyme)

As well as being a key ingredient of any self-respecting herb garden, thyme definitely deserves a place on a large rockery. Since some species spread to form a dense mat of 2ft or more, it does need plenty of space but it is worth making room for it just for the opportunity to rub your hands through the deliciously aromatic foliage. This is particularly true of lemon thyme, where one brush of the hand to reveal that divine citrus fragrance can transport you instantly to the Bay of Naples.

Thyme is a willing grower, given full sun and well-drained soil, and produces clusters of flowers in shades of red, pink or white. Some varieties have the bonus of variegated foliage. The only attention it needs once established is a light clip with a pair of shears after flowering to remove the old flower heads and to keep the plant looking tidy. These are among the best varieties to grow:

T. citriodorus **'Doone Valley'** is a lemon thyme with pink flowers borne on mats of lovely dark-green leaves with yellow variegation that give off a fabulous citrus scent. Height 6in, spread 2ft.

T. citriodorus **'Silver Queen'** is a bushier lemon thyme that has dark-green-and-white variegated foliage, masses of pale-mauve flowers, and that wonderful lemon aroma. Height 8in, spread 10in.

T. serpyllum is a lower-growing species of thyme, making it excellent for tumbling over rocks or drystone walls. *T. serpyllum* **'Albus'** has white flowers on aromatic, mid-green leaves, **'Annie Hall'** is pale pink, **'Coccineus'** is reddish-purple and **'Pink Chintz'** is deep pink. Height 3in, spread 2ft. If space is short – or if you are looking for a thyme to plant in a container – try the slow-growing *T. serpyllum* **'Elfin'**, which lives up to its name by forming rosy-pink flowers on a tight bun of dark-green leaves. Height 2in, spread 6in.

Likes Well-drained soil, full sun.

Flowering season June–July.

Key points Strongly scented foliage, often variegated, leaves can be used in cooking. Pretty flowers.

VFM 9

Veronica prostrata (Rock Speedwell)

All too often, speedwell is an unwelcome garden visitor, growing as a weed in a lawn, but the cultivated semi-evergreen form is a useful rock plant, quickly forming mats of pretty blue, pink or white flowers. It can still be invasive, however, spreading to almost 2ft, so you will either need to give it plenty of room or keep it in check by trimming it back after flowering.

The flowers are carried on erect 6in spikes above a carpet of green leaves, the common dark-blue form benefiting from its distinctive white eye. *V. prostrata* **'Blue Mirror'** is a good dark blue, but more eye-catching is **'Trehane'**, which has royal-blue flowers set off by golden-yellow leaves. Another attractive foliage variety is *V. prostrata* **'Goldwell'** (aka **'Verbrig'**), which has dark-blue flowers and variegated golden leaves. For a paler blue, try **'Spode Blue'**, or you could also opt for **'Mrs Holt'** (pink), **'Lilac Time'** (lilac) or **'Alba'** (white). Given reasonable drainage and a position in sun or light shade, you should have no problems growing rock speedwell.

Likes Reasonably drained soil in sun or light shade.
Flowering season May–July.
Key points Tough, unfussy, fast growing, pretty flowers. Some varieties have golden foliage.
VFM 8

PART III

Bulbs

Every garden should feature a selection of bulbs, for nothing does more to lift the spirits than the sight of the first snowdrops, crocuses and daffodils – a sure sign that the dark days of winter are nearly over and that spring in all its beauty is just around the corner.

Many species are easy to grow, low maintenance and offer outstanding value for money because not only do they return year after year, they multiply. Within a few years, what started out as a single bulb will have expanded to a magnificent clump. The two main things to remember are to make sure that the bulbs are planted deep enough (in a hole roughly three times the height of the bulb itself) and to resist the temptation to remove the foliage after flowering until it has died down completely. Bulbs use their leaves to create energy for producing next year's flowers, so if you hack off – or even tie up – the foliage while it is still green, you are depriving the bulb of essential food.

Most bulbs are cheap and readily available in early autumn from garden shops or market stalls. Try to purchase good-sized bulbs, and at planting time add a handful of horticultural grit to improve drainage at the bottom of the hole and a little bonemeal to provide nutrients. If you garden on cold, heavy soils, growing tulips will prove an uphill struggle, but luckily there are plenty of other pretty bulbs that can cope with the very worst of the UK climate.

Convallaria majalis (Lily of the Valley)

If you need a reliable groundcover plant for a moist, shady spot – and one that will lift the whole area with a fragrance that has captivated writers for centuries – look no further than lily of the valley. The small, pendent white bells that are borne in groups on 8in stems above large green leaves may look as delicate as their perfume suggests, but the plants themselves are deceptively tough. They will grow in any soil (provided it retains some moisture), and will even tolerate full shade, although they may not bloom as profusely there. So give them a partially shaded location under trees or shrubs and soon they will turn that area of your garden into a natural woodland. The only problem is, they don't quite know when to stop. Spreading rapidly via underground rhizomes, they can easily cover an area of 25 sq ft, in the process swamping everything in their path. If you have treasured, less sturdy plants in the vicinity, watch out for the new lily of the valley shoots emerging above ground in spring and dig them up – rhizomes and all. It will do no damage to the rest of the clump, but will at least keep the invading hordes at bay for the time being.

Lilies of the valley are best bought as small clumps in pots from garden centres or online retailers in the same way as other border perennials, and it is worth adding some leaf mould or garden compost when planting, to give them a good start. After that, you can just sit back and wait for that fragrance. Once established, they will produce so many flowers that you will be able to cut off some stems for arranging indoors in a small vase, filling the room with the unmistakable scent known by French perfumiers as *muguet des bois*.

Likes Moist soil in partial shade.
Flowering season April–May.
Key points Amazing fragrance, good groundcover for difficult areas.
VFM 8

Crocosmia crocosmiiflora (Montbretia)

A scan through the varieties of crocosmia for sale at most garden outlets reveals an impressive array of named cultivars in red, orange and yellow, such as **'Lucifer'** (fiery red), **'Emily Mckenzie'** (orange with red blotches) and **'George Davison'** (yellow). These are well worth growing if you have a sheltered, sunny spot and well-drained soil, but otherwise they may perish in the harshest of winters. A much tougher form is the common, native montbretia, which has equally attractive sprays of bright, reddish-orange flowers but is far less fussy about soil conditions or position, even thriving in partial shade.

Although it originated in southern Africa, it is sufficiently hardy to grow wild in the Western Isles of Scotland. The gently arching stems rise to a height of about 2ft, making it an excellent subject for the front or middle of a border, but it will grow equally well in dry or wet soil and even under large shrubs or in neglected corners of the garden. The grassy, green leaves will quickly spread to cover 3ft or more, but you can easily control the clump by digging up outer portions after flowering and replanting them in another part of the garden.

Montbretia can be purchased as individual corms or as small clumps. Better still, if your neighbour has a patch, he or she will probably be only too glad to give some away. They need no special care and, unlike other bulbs, do not even resent having their still-green foliage chopped back by half in the autumn to keep it looking tidy. Just in case the winter is unduly harsh, leave several inches of brown foliage on the plant to protect it from severe frosts. This can be removed in the spring when the new green shoots start to emerge.

Likes Any soil in full sun or partial shade.
Flowering season July–September.
Key points Grows almost anywhere, long-lived, bright-orange flowers.
Easy to divide for extra plants.
VFM 9

Crocus

There are ninety different species of crocus, but for the purposes of the gardener they can be divided into two distinct groups: those that flower in the spring and those that flower in the autumn. The spring-blooming species are the most widely grown, and frankly no garden should be without these lovely little perennials whose large, cup-shaped flowers in purple, blue, yellow or white burst open at the first sign of spring sunshine to show off their bright orange stamens. They are so cheap to buy, require hardly any care, and will reward you by forming sizeable clumps within just a couple of years. The time to plant spring crocuses is in September or October (for autumn crocuses, see overleaf). You can allow them to naturalise at the front of borders, on rockeries or even in the lawn. (If you do plant the bulbs in grass, remember not to cut the lawn until the leaves have died back.)

To plant crocuses, dig a shallow trench about 4in deep and wide enough so that you can fit in at least half a dozen bulbs. Like all bulbs, crocuses look best in drifts rather than planted individually. Sprinkle a layer of horticultural grit into the bottom of the trench to improve drainage, add a little bonemeal or general fertiliser and place the bulbs (growing side up) on the bed of grit about 3in apart. Then carefully fill in the trench with the displaced soil. If there are large clumps of earth, break these up so that the little shoots don't face too much of a battle to reach the surface. In spring, the flowers will emerge at around the same time as the green leaves with their central, silver stripes.

There are so many types of spring crocus you will be spoilt for choice. The most familiar – and the ones usually sold by supermarkets, greengrocers and on market stalls – are the large-flowered Dutch hybrids. They grow to a height of around 4in, and include **'Remembrance'** (purple), **'Queen of the Blues'** (blue), **'Flower Record'** (violet-mauve), **'Golden Mammoth'** (yellow), **'Jeanne d'Arc'** (white) and **'Pickwick'** (lilac-and-purple striped). However, there are many other spring species that are just as easy to grow. Look out for *C. angustifolius* (yellow and bronze), *C. chrysanthus* **'Blue Peter'** (pale blue with a darker blotch), *C. chrysanthus* **'Cream Beauty'** (cream), *C. chrysanthus* **'Ladykiller'** (purple and white), *C. minimus* (violet with a yellow throat), *C. sieberi* **'Albus'** (one of the earliest varieties to bloom, white with a yellow throat), *C. sieberi* **'Hubert Edelsten'** (purple and white), *C. sieberi sublimis* **'Tricolor'** (an unusual form with three distinct colour bands: purple, white and yellow) and *C. tommasinianus* (lavender-mauve).

The autumn-flowering species should be planted in July. There are fewer to choose from, but *C. speciosus* contains some pretty hybrids with goblet-shaped flowers, including **'Conqueror'** (purple), **'Oxonian'** (violet-blue) and **'Albus'** (white).

Likes Any well-drained soil in sun or light shade.
Flowering season February–April (spring crocus), September–November (autumn crocus).
Key points Cheap to buy, easy to grow, soon forms large clumps of cheerful flowers.
VFM 10

Galanthus (Snowdrop)

In many gardens the delightful, pendulous flowers of snowdrops are the first to appear each year. Peering through the ground from January, they are invaluable for providing winter interest before ultimately giving way to crocuses and narcissi. They are not quite as accommodating as those two but, given the right conditions, will spread to form magical clumps of white beneath trees or shrubs.

Snowdrop bulbs should be planted about 4in deep and 3in apart in groups in September or October. Choose a location that receives some shade and where the soil will not be baked dry by summer sun. Incorporate some leaf mould into the soil, dig a small trench (as with crocuses) and stand the bulbs on a layer of horticultural grit. This is the most cost-effective way of growing snowdrops. Some experts recommend planting them 'in the green' (while they are still in leaf after flowering), but this method is rather more expensive and, in my experience, offers no greater guarantee of success. Any snowdrop clumps that become too crowded can be lifted and divided immediately after flowering.

The common snowdrop is *Galanthus nivalis*, and this is the species that is most readily available (although specialist growers have all manner of costly rarities to choose from). *G. nivalis* **'Magnet'** is a vigorous grower bearing pure white flowers, the inner petals of which are shaded dark green. It has 8in-high stems, as does *G. nivalis* **'S. Arnott'**, which has larger flowers. There is also a double form, *G. nivalis* **'Flore Pleno'**, which only grows about 4in tall. The novice gardener is certainly advised to stick to the common snowdrop (ten bulbs should set you back no more than £1.50), bearing in mind that bulbs of the more exotic species have been known to change hands for £100 apiece.

Likes Moist, well-drained soil and light shade.

Flowering season January–March.

Key points Winter interest, inexpensive, easily divided to form new clumps.

VFM 8

Iris hollandica (Dutch Iris)

There are a number of species of garden iris, from tall border perennials to dwarf rockery specimens, but the former are fairly high maintenance and the latter tend to be short-lived on anything but light, chalky soil. Summer-flowering Dutch irises are far more amenable and will put on a vibrant show in colours as diverse as bronze, silver-blue, dark red, yellow, purple and white without taking up much space in the border. They grow to little more than 2ft in height, and even after a few years will only have spread to form a clump about 10in in width.

The flowers themselves are simply breathtaking, a photographer's dream. Many varieties have contrasting upper and lower petals (such as navy blue and bronze or mauve and burgundy), complete with vivid yellow centres for added effect. They may look exotic, but they are the easiest of plants to grow and are totally hardy. Plant them in groups in a sunny spot in September or October about 6in deep and a similar distance apart. Add a layer of horticultural grit at the base of the planting hole and sprinkle in a little fertiliser. In mild conditions, the narrow leaves may appear before the onset of winter, but the flowers still won't follow until late May or June. After flowering, deadhead but leave the foliage on until it has completely died down. In late summer, while the foliage is still green, you can give the plants a liquid feed to boost them for the following year.

In view of the fact that they will come back bigger and better year after year they are extremely good value. A pack of thirty will cost you between £4 and £7 depending on the variety, the more unusual bi-colours tending to cost more than the purples, yellows and whites. Look out for **'Black Beauty'** (navy blue, bronze and yellow), **'Blue Pearl'** (royal blue with a yellow throat), **'Bronze Beauty'** (purple, amber, bronze and yellow), **'Purple Sensation'** (purple with a yellow throat), **'Red Ember'** (red, brown and yellow), **'Sapphire Beauty'** (royal blue and sky blue with a yellow throat), **'Silvery Beauty'** (pale blue, white and yellow), **'Symphony'** (white and yellow with an orange throat) and **'White Wedgwood'** (white with a yellow throat). Alternatively, you will find that bags of mixed Dutch Iris bulbs represent even better value.

Likes Reasonably drained soil, full sun.
Flowering season May–July.
Key points Magnificent flowers like works of art. Low maintenance and will come back bigger and better, year after year.
VFM 10

Muscari (Grape Hyacinth)

The humble grape hyacinth would never win any prizes in a spring-bulb beauty contest. The foliage is straggly and, compared to crocuses, snowdrops and narcissi, its dense spikes of small, blue, bell-shaped flowers are fairly unremarkable. However, it does provide a useful source of true blue after all those early spring yellows and whites, it is extremely easy to grow and it spreads rapidly, enabling you to lift and divide every few years in late summer so that you can sprinkle its virtues all around the garden.

Muscari bulbs should be planted in September or October in groups about 3in deep and 3in apart. Add a little horticultural grit at planting time. The species most often seen in gardens is *M. armeniacum*, a vigorous grower that reaches a height of 8in and has mid-blue flowers. A less invasive form is the 5in-tall *M. aucheri* **'Blue Magic'**, which has royal-blue flowers. If you want something different from the standard blue, try *M. armeniacum* **'Valerie Finnis'** (sky-blue flowers), *M. latifolium*, a 6in-tall, two-tone form whose spikes are dark blue topped with paler blue, or *M. azureum*, which grows to a height of 6in and has stouter-shaped flowers in a lighter shade of Cambridge blue with darker veining. There is also a white version, *M. azureum* **'Album'**.

Likes Reasonably drained soil in full sun or light shade.
Flowering season April–May.
Key points Fast growing, low maintenance, easily divided to form more clumps, a splash of spring blue.
VFM 8

Narcissus (Daffodil)

If there is one garden flower that I would class as indispensable, it is the narcissus. Even on the dullest of spring days, they emit pockets of sunshine, and when the skies are blue . . . well, you can understand why Wordsworth was so inspired. Yet all it takes to create your own 'host of golden daffodils' is a few pounds and the minimum of maintenance. When people think of narcissi, they often focus on the familiar, tall, yellow daffodil swaying gently in the breeze, but the genus has so much more to offer. Sure, there are the plain yellow daffodils with their large trumpets, but you can also buy border varieties with contrasting orange, red, peach or pink coronas (centres), whites with orange cups, flamboyant doubles, unusual flowers with split coronas, delicate jonquils with several blooms on each stem, and beautiful miniatures that grow to no more than 6in tall and are just perfect for rockeries and containers.

Whatever type of narcissus you grow, the rules are simple. Plant the bulbs from late August until the end of September into a hole, the depth of which should be at least three times the height of the actual bulb. So for a 2in bulb, dig a hole at least 6in deep. Failure to plant deeply enough will result in 'blind' specimens, where the leaves come up but produce no flowers. Deep planting also helps to prevent taller varieties – particularly heavy-headed doubles – from being flattened by spring gusts, whereupon their prone flowers will inevitably be mangled by slugs. Add horticultural grit and a little fertiliser to the hole and plant any large bulbs up to 10in apart. Smaller, dwarf narcissi can be spaced just a couple of inches apart. Replace the earth, taking care not to knock the bulbs onto their sides as you do so. After flowering, remove the dead blooms in order to channel essential nutrients down to the bulb but leave the foliage on until it has died off completely and turned brown. The dying foliage may look unsightly, but if you plan your garden so that daffodils are planted in among summer-flowering shrubs or perennials, the leaves from these will hide it from public view until it can safely be removed from July onwards. Do not be tempted to tie the foliage in a knot as this, too, will harm the following year's display. You can give them a liquid feed after flowering, but that is the only attention they need. Just leave them undisturbed and watch them multiply year upon year.

You can buy bags of mixed or named varieties from reputable market stalls in August, but first check that the bulbs are healthy and of a good size (taller varieties should be at least 4in in circumference), because bigger bulbs produce more flowers. There are hundreds of narcissi to choose from, and by mixing early and late varieties you will be able to extend the season of interest from the end of winter right through spring. These are some of the best taller specimens for borders:

N. **'Avalon'** is a tall variety with elegant, pale yellow flowers fading to white at the centre and a pale-yellow cup. Height 18in. **March–May.**

N. **'Chanterelle'** bears unusual flat blooms of golden yellow with white edging to the outer petals. Height 18in. **March–April.**

N. **'Cheerfulness'** has 16in-tall, slender, erect stems, each topped with as many as four fragrant, double, creamy-white flowers with yellow centres. *N.* **'Yellow Cheerfulness'** has fragrant, double, lemon-yellow flowers. Both are truly exceptional additions to the garden. **March–April.**

N. **'Dick Wilden'** has large, fully double, sulphur-yellow flowers with frilly centres on sturdy stems. These make good cut flowers. Height 15in. **April–May.**

N. **'Geranium'** produces clusters of up to six fragrant, single, white flowers with bright orange cups on 14in stems. **March–April.**

N. **'Ice Follies'** has white petals around a large, frilly-edged, primrose-yellow cup which fades to white as it ages. A fast-growing, early and prolific bloomer. Height 16in. **Feb–March.**

N. **'Katie Heath'** is a new later-flowering introduction sporting fragrant, single, white petals around an attractive apricot-pink cup. Height 14in. **April–May.**

N. **'King Alfred'** is the traditional golden daffodil, an old favourite with rich yellow blooms and a prominent yellow trumpet. Height 16in. March–April.

N. **'Lemon Beauty'** is a split corona daffodil that produces pure white blooms with a star-shaped yellow flash in the centre – like a lemon meringue pie. Height 18in. March–April.

N. **'Orangery'** has creamy-white outer petals and a large flat corona of orange and yellow. Height 18in. March–April.

N. poeticus var. recurvus **'Pheasant's Eye'** is an old variety producing highly scented, single, white flowers with small, red-rimmed, yellow cups. Height 14in. March–May.

N. **'Replete'** is one for those looking for something different. It has 4in-wide, double flowers with white outer petals surrounding a ruffled cup of peachy-pink. Height 18in. March–April.

N. **'Sailboat'** is an exquisite jonquil where each 12in stem carries up to three sweetly scented flowers that have creamy-white petals around a primrose-yellow cup. March–April.

N. **'Suzy'** is a highly fragrant jonquil producing pairs of pale-yellow flowers around flared, orange cups. Height 16in. April–May.

N. **'Tahiti'** is a delightful double form, bearing 4in-wide blooms that have lemon-yellow outer petals arranged around orange inner petals – an eye-catching combination. Height 18in. March–April.

N. **'Trepolo'** is an unusual but highly desirable variety with a split corona from which orange streaks radiate out across the white, rounded outer petals. Height 14in. March–April.

Here are some of the choicest dwarf narcissi:

N. bulbocodium **'Golden Bells'** is commonly known as the 'Hoop Petticoat Daffodil' on account of its enlarged, golden trumpets. A vigorous grower, it reaches a height of 7in. March–April.

N. **'Jack Snipe'** is a fast-growing miniature that produces masses of flowers with white petals around prominent, bright-yellow trumpets. Height 9in. March–April.

N. **'Jenny'** has graceful, creamy-white petals that arch backwards as if they were in a wind tunnel. They surround a prominent, crimped trumpet of lemon yellow that fades to creamy-white as it ages. Height 9in. **March–April.**

N. **'Jetfire'** produces yellow flowers with bright-orange trumpets. Height 6in. **March–April.**

N. **'Minnow'** has clusters of dainty, fragrant, creamy-white flowers with contrasting lemon-yellow cups, borne on 6in stems. **March–April.**

N. **'Reggae'** produces white flowers with a lovely pink trumpet. Height 6in. **March–April.**

N. **'Sun Disc'** is a fragrant, miniature jonquil with pretty, rounded, pale-yellow petals and flattened, darker yellow cups, the overall flower resembling the shape of a large button. Each stem carries several blooms. Height 7in. **April–May.**

N. **'Tête-à-Tête'** is one of the most popular dwarf varieties and is particularly suitable for growing in pots. An early flowerer, it produces multiple golden-yellow flowers with darker yellow trumpets on 6in stems. **Feb–April.**

Likes Well-drained soil in sun or partial shade.
Flowering season February–May.
Key points Flowers come in a huge range of colours and shapes, essential spring colour, easy to grow, low maintenance, will improve year after year. Some have lovely fragrance.
VFM 10

Scilla siberica (Siberian Squill)

The Spanish bluebell (known either as *Scilla hispanica* or *Hyacinthoides hispanica*) is a really easy bulb to grow and, as well as a rather insipid blue, can be found in pink or white. However, not only does it rapidly become invasive – primarily because it thrives absolutely anywhere – but it is also threatening to wipe out the native English bluebell. It is very much the 'grey squirrel' of the bulb world.

Predictably, the English bluebell (*Hyacinthoides non-scripta*) is much fussier about soil conditions and can take several years to become established, so a more reliable alternative to the Spanish invader may be *Scilla siberica*, the Siberian squill, a lovely little plant with narrow, strap-shaped, glossy green leaves and dainty 8in spikes of bright-blue, nodding, bell-shaped flowers. *S. siberica* **'Spring Beauty'** has vivid, deep-blue flowers, and there is also a white form, *S. siberica var. alba*. Plant the bulbs in groups about 4in deep and 4in apart in August or September. Add horticultural grit to improve the drainage and some leaf mould or rotted compost to help retain moisture. Siberian squills are easy to grow, extremely hardy and are ideal for naturalising in drifts in semi-shaded spots beneath deciduous shrubs. Although they should soon form healthy colonies, they never become invasive – unlike the Spanish bluebell.

Likes Reasonably drained, moist soil in sun or partial shade.
Flowering season March–April.
Key points Small, blue spring flowers, non-invasive.
VFM 8

PART IV

Annuals and biennials

By their very nature, annuals and biennials should be plants that definitely *will* die in your garden. Annuals are plants that only live for a year and biennials produce flowers in their second year and then die . . . and in 99.9 per cent of cases this is true. However, there is one annual genus that, with a little care, is so hardy it can be treated as a perennial; and another annual and one biennial that self-seed so freely they, too, will come back year after year. All three are easy to grow and are therefore well worth considering in the quest for indestructible plants.

Limnanthes douglasii (Poached Egg Plant)

From a distance, a bank covered in *Limnanthes douglasii* looks like the biggest carpet of primroses you have ever seen. On closer inspection the large, saucer-shaped flowers of this low-growing annual are actually two-tone: bright-yellow centres with white edges, hence its common name of the poached egg plant. The lightly fragrant, showy flowers are produced in profusion throughout summer 6in above fleshy, fern-like, yellow-green leaves, but instead of just dying out after flowering (like most other annuals), the poached egg plant self-seeds so freely that dozens of replacement plants will return year after year, providing you with an even bigger carpet of colour – all for the price of a packet of seeds.

As hardy annuals, the seeds should be sown shallowly (about 3mm deep) in March or early April directly into the spot where they are to flower. Rake over a patch of ground in a sunny position until it is free of weeds and any clumps of earth have been broken down into a fine tilth. Scatter the seeds and lightly cover them with soil or multi-purpose compost. Water them in, using a watering can with a fine rose. As the seedlings emerge, thin them out to about 4in apart, and continue to water gently during dry spells. After flowering, don't dig the plants up – simply leave them in place to self-seed for the following year. In this way, it can be treated as a perennial. The poached egg plant makes excellent groundcover, each plant spreading to 1ft or more, will thrive even on heavy clay, and is also attractive to bees and hoverflies.

Likes Any soil, full sun.
Flowering season June–September.
Key points Tough, long flowering season, good groundcover, attractive to insects. Self-seeds freely, giving a colourful display year after year.
VFM 9

Myosotis sylvatica (Forget-me-not)

Strictly speaking, forget-me-nots are biennials but, like the poached egg plant, they self-seed with such abandon that they can be used as perennials. You can either sow the seeds in May or June directly into the border where they are to grow for flowering the following year or you can buy small plants in the autumn – often in packs of six from market stalls. These, too, will bloom the following spring and – if you just leave them in place – for successive years after that in ever-greater numbers.

Forget-me-nots have grey-green leaves that are smothered in clusters of flowers, each with a tiny yellow eye. Azure blue is the traditional colour of *Myosotis sylvatica*, but each plant also carries flower heads of a darker blue as well as some that are pink or lavender. The colour variation adds to the charm of this most appealing of woodland wild flowers. You may also be able to find a true dark-blue variety (*M. sylvatica* **'Indigo Blue'**) and strains in pink (*M. sylvatica* **'Victoria Pink'**) or white (*M. sylvatica* **'Snowsylva'**). Planted in a moist but reasonably drained spot either in full sun or partial shade, they will quickly naturalise to create a dense 1ft-high drift that provides essential May colour in between spring bulbs and summer perennials or annuals. The only attention they require is to be watered during hot, dry weather. Once you have allowed forget-me-nots to seed themselves in your garden, you will never be without them – but nor would you want to be.

Likes Moist but reasonably drained soil in sun or partial shade.
Flowering season April–May.
Key points Lovely spring colour, self-seeds freely to make extra plants that will come back year after year.
VFM 9

Pelargonium (Geranium)

Unless you have a greenhouse or cold frame and can therefore grow everything from seed, fitting out your garden with summer bedding plants can be an expensive business, especially as you have to throw them out and start all over again the following year. But with pelargoniums this does not have to be the case because, in return for just a little winter care, they will come back for several years like true perennials.

Pelargoniums are sometimes incorrectly called geraniums, but real geraniums are the hardy types dealt with in the earlier section on herbaceous perennials. The principal form is the zonal pelargonium – so-called because of the dark, zonal marking on the leaf – and, in a range of reds, pinks, salmons, oranges, whites (and, more recently, yellows), it is a mainstay of borders, containers and municipal gardens. There are also trailing pelargoniums, notably the form which has brittle, ivy-shaped leaves and is ideal for hanging baskets. Meanwhile, the splendid, upright, regal pelargonium has large flowers in red, purple, pink or white, usually with handsome, darker blotches. Not only are these plants all exceptionally free flowering over a long period (as you would expect from an annual), they are also a godsend for the gardener who wants to go away on holiday in summer. For pelargoniums are drought tolerant and can go several weeks without the need for watering. In fact, the surest way to kill a pelargonium is to overwater it. Furthermore, unlike some other popular summer bedding plants such as marigolds, dahlias and petunias, pelargoniums will not be stripped bare by marauding slugs and snails.

The plants can be grown from seed but are most easily raised via small plug plants bought in late spring from any reputable garden retailer. Around the end of May (when all risk of frost has passed) plant them out about 1ft apart in a sunny spot in ground that has been improved with fertiliser, give them the occasional liquid feed, then just sit back and enjoy their spectacular summer display for weeks and months on end. Unless winter comes early, they will often still be flowering well into November but, whereas you will then be throwing your old zinnias, lobelia and marigolds on the compost heap, you can dig up your pelargoniums to save for next year. Simply put each plant in an individual pot, fill with multi-purpose compost and cut back the stems to about half. If you have a sunny porch or conservatory or a light windowsill in an unheated room, you can keep them indoors over winter; if not, find a sheltered spot in the garden and cover the pots with a couple of layers of fleece. There is no need to water them at all over winter. The following March, cut back any straggly growth so that the plant has a nice compact shape (stems should ideally be pruned to just above a strong, new green shoot), remove the fleece from the outdoor specimens and give them some water. As they grow, continue to water and feed every couple of weeks. Keep an eye on the weather forecast in case a late frost requires the reinstatement of the fleece. By late April/early May they can all be placed outdoors to harden off in readiness for planting out at the end of the month. Plug plants can work out at as little as twenty pence each, which is not bad value for a plant that may survive for five years or more. Plants can either be bought as mixed colours, which usually proves cheaper, or as named varieties.

Zonal pelargoniums reach a height of 12–18in. Excellent varieties include **'Apple Blossom'** (single lilac-pink flowers), **'Americana White'** (single white), **'Calliope Dark Red'** (large, semi-double dark red), **'Custard Cream'** (single yellow), **'Flower Fairy White Splash'** (semi-double white flowers with a large pink eye), **'Mrs Pollock'** (single orange flowers with variegated foliage), **'Octavia Hill'** (large, single, scarlet flowers), **'Tango Neon Purple'** (double magenta) and **'Tango Salmon'** (double salmon).

Among the best ivy-leaf trailing varieties (height 18in, spread 2ft) are **'Blue Sybil'** (double, rosebud-style, lavender flowers), **'Mexica Ruby'** (semi-double red-and-white striped flowers), **'Tommy'** (double, deep-burgundy flowers) and **'White Pearl Sybil'** (double, rosebud-style, white flowers).

Classic regal pelargoniums (height 20in) include **'Aristo Black Beauty'** (dark-red-wine flowers with a lighter picotee edging), **'Aristo Darling'** (pink and burgundy bicolour), **'Aristo Petticoat'** (white, pale lilac and deep purple) and **'Regalia Lavender'** (lavender-pink with darker blotches).

Likes Reasonably drained soil in full sun or light shade.
Flowering season June–November.
Key points Free flowering well into late autumn, drought tolerant. Easily overwintered so that they can be kept for several years.
VFM 9

PART V

Ornamental grasses

Ornamental grasses can play a vital role in the garden, either planted in containers or in borders, where their flower heads, foliage and structure complement the more vibrant colours of herbaceous perennials. There are grasses for any situation and in every shape or size, ranging from 10in dwarfs to monsters over 10ft. The taller species look particularly effective on a breezy day, when their presence has a definite calming effect, and those with coloured leaves give a long season of interest.

Make sure you select a variety that is completely hardy (for example, the popular pampas grass, *Cortaderia selloana*, is not guaranteed to survive winter in colder parts of the UK), and save money by purchasing a small plant and watching it grow over the years.

Carex elata 'Aurea' (Bowles' Golden Sedge)

With its tufts of slender, arching, gold-and-green-striped leaves, this compact grass loves moist, moderately fertile conditions and is therefore ideal for a bog garden, the front of a damp, partially shaded border or the margins of a pond. It grows to a height of around 2ft 6in with a spread of 18in, and although it carries small spikes of dark brown flowers in early summer, it is grown pretty much exclusively for its foliage, which catches the sun and positively glows in shade. It is semi-evergreen, but any dead or tired leaves should be removed in the spring. You can do this by pulling out the dead, brown sections by hand, but remember to wear gardening gloves because blades of ornamental grass are often sharp and can deliver nasty cuts. If you need to cut it back hard because the clump as a whole is looking jaded, do so after flowering.

This is essentially a low-maintenance, disease-free, ornamental grass. It can be divided in spring every few years if you want to reduce its size or simply create more plants.

Likes Moist soil in partial shade.
Flowering season May–June.
Key points Golden foliage all year round, compact, tolerates heavy clay.
VFM 7

Helictotrichon sempervirens (Blue Oat Grass)

Generally regarded as the easiest of all the blue grasses, blue oat grass forms a neat 2ft-high mound of stiff, blue-grey leaves that are topped with 4ft-tall, upright, golden spikelets in mid-summer. In all but the harshest winters it remains evergreen, so the stunning foliage retains its colour all year round. It needs little maintenance – indeed your only chore will be to remove the old flowering stems along with any dead leaves in spring. To achieve the best colour, grow it in a sunny spot in well-drained – even poor – soil. Once established, it can cope with drought conditions, but if grown in heavy, wet ground and too much shade, the foliage may be prone to rust. If your garden is borderline between the two, choose the sunniest, driest spot available and add plenty of horticultural grit into the planting hole.

Blue oat grass is totally hardy and will spread to over 2ft 6in, forming an impressive architectural feature in either a herbaceous border or a gravel garden. For the best effect, try planting it in groups of three. If the clumps become too large, they can be lifted and divided in spring to create extra plants. *H. sempervirens* **'Sapphire'** (aka **'Saphirsprudel'**) is a useful cultivar, boasting enhanced blue leaves and having improved resistance to rust.

Likes Well-drained soil in full sun or light shade.

Flowering season June–August.

Key points Blue leaves all year round, happy in poor soil. Drought tolerant when established.

VFM 8

Miscanthus sinensis 'Zebrinus' (Zebra Grass)

Native to Japan, this popular old grass takes its name from the distinctive, horizontal, creamy-yellow bands on its bright-green leaves. It grows to a height of 5ft and a spread of 3ft, but its gently arching leaves give it a more relaxed, natural habit than some stiff, upright grasses. It is unfussy about soil – so long as drainage is adequate – but prefers a position that receives a little shade as the bands may scorch in full sun. If the summer has been hot, in August zebra grass will produce silky spikes of pale-pink, fan-shaped flowers. These are followed by silvery seed heads which help to maintain interest through winter (the leaves are deciduous and die down).

Zebra grass makes a superb backdrop for summer border perennials, is completely hardy, easy to grow and requires little maintenance. The old stems should be cut back to the ground in late winter or early spring before the new shoots appear.

Likes Any free-draining soil in sun or light shade.
Flowering season August–September.
Key points Attractive, variegated cream bands on leaves. Good backdrop for summer flowers.
VFM 7

Stipa gigantea (Golden Oats or Giant Feather Grass)

Golden oats makes a real statement at the back of a border, its feathery, oat-like flower heads rising gracefully above clumps of slender, grey-green leaves. These flower heads start off purplish-green before maturing to a golden colour, their shade and texture making them popular in dried-flower arrangements. It is an excellent plant for introducing movement into a large border as it sways and shimmers freely, even on days when there is only a light breeze. It can reach a height of 8ft and a spread of 4ft, so it requires plenty of space to be seen to full advantage. It is evergreen, so provides winter interest and needs little care, apart from removing any dead foliage in spring. It likes well-drained soil in full sun, so if your soil needs improving, add plenty of horticultural grit at planting time. This grass will definitely not thank you for being planted in wet soil or in shade.

For a slightly more compact form, try *S. gigantea* **'Goldilocks'**, which only grows to a height of just over 5ft.

Likes Well-drained soil, full sun.

Flowering season June–July.

Key points Tall, back-of-the-border grass with elegant, swaying flower heads. Good for dried-flower arrangements.

VFM 7

PART VI

Conifers

Conifers have acquired something of a bad name in recent years due largely to one species, *Cuprocyparis leylandii,* whose rapid, vigorous growth (if left untamed, it will reach a height of 100ft) has resulted in many a dispute between neighbours. The biggest, single mistake people make with conifers is planting them too close to a boundary or house. They spot a 2ft-high specimen at a garden centre, are told it is slow growing, and ten years later find they have created a monster that blocks out half the light.

When buying a conifer it is essential to choose the right sort for its intended position. This should not be difficult as there are more than 600 species to choose from, and most are evergreen, giving year-round interest. There are dwarf forms, spreading types, species with attractive blue or golden foliage and conifers with seed-cones that will attract birds to the garden. Every garden should have at least one – but make sure it is the *right* one.

Abies balsamea 'Nana' (Dwarf Balsam Fir)

This dwarf, evergreen North American conifer has a neat, rounded growth habit, its densely packed, soft, dark-green needles being carried on horizontal, spreading branches. Each year's new growth comes in the shape of a small ball at the end of each shoot and is a lovely lime-green colour, contrasting nicely with the older foliage. The tree eventually reaches a height of about 2ft and a spread of 3ft, but because it grows at a rate of little more than an inch per year it is an ideal low-maintenance specimen for borders or even rock gardens.

It grows in any soil – even clay – but likes some protection from the full heat of the summer sun, so is best planted in a semi-shaded spot. Its tidy green foliage, which has the fragrance of balsam, looks fresh all year round, but you may need to water it in prolonged periods of drought. The only other attention it requires is the removal of any dead branches from time to time, but the addition of some leaf mould, manure or rotted garden compost at planting time and a late winter mulch around the base of the plant will help to retain moisture during the summer. Given the right conditions, dwarf balsam fir can be expected to live for fifty years or more.

Likes Any soil in partial shade.
Key points Slow growing, compact. Fragrant foliage, brightly contrasting new shoots, happy on clay. Long-lived.
VFM 9

Chamaecyparis pisifera 'Sungold' (False Cypress)

This dwarf evergreen conifer has thin, yellow-to-lime-green needles and a loose, weeping habit, making it a useful focal point in a smaller garden. The young shoots are golden and it retains its colour well throughout winter. It will eventually form a mound with a height and spread of 10ft, but it grows so slowly that this can take thirty years or more; its growth can also be restricted by occasional pruning. It is unfussy about soil provided the site drains fairly well without being too dry, so add rotted compost at planting time and give it an annual spring mulch to retain some moisture through summer. Once established, it can cope with drought, but would probably appreciate not being put to the test.

It tolerates some shade, but for the best foliage colour plant it in full sun as, unlike some other golden-leaved cultivars in the species, it is not prone to leaf scorch. However, a sheltered position, with a fence or a large shrub to act as a windbreak, would be beneficial in order to prevent any risk of windburn in winter storms.

Likes Any reasonably drained soil in sun or light shade; prefers a sheltered spot out of strong winds.
Key points Slow-growing, mound-forming evergreen with golden foliage for year-round interest. Long-lived.
VFM 9

Juniperus squamata 'Blue Star'

Slow-growing dwarf conifers look very much at home on rock gardens, where they provide some necessary height, their structure can be seen at its best without being obscured by large plants and where their evergreen foliage offers year-round colour and interest. This juniper is one of the best rockery varieties. It has a dense, spreading habit and its branches bear aromatic, pointed, blue-grey leaves and oval-shaped, black cones. The new spring growth is an intense powder blue, allowing it to stand out from the older shoots. It thrives in any reasonably drained soil – including chalk or sand – is happy in partial shade and reaches an eventual height (after twenty years) of no more than 18in with a spread of 3ft. It requires little or no pruning, but if you do need to remove any dead branches wear gardening gloves: the needle-like leaves are sharp, and contact with the foliage may irritate your skin.

If you are looking for a slightly larger variety, try *J. squamata* **'Blue Carpet'**, an outstanding blue groundcover juniper which reaches a similar height to 'Blue Star' but will eventually spread to cover 7ft or more.

Likes Any reasonably drained soil in full sun or partial shade.
Key points Slow growing, compact, evergreen, blue-grey foliage for year-round interest. Black cones, long-lived.
VFM 9

Thuja occidentalis 'Smaragd' (White Cedar)

'Smaragd' is a slow-growing variety of evergreen white cedar with a tight habit and a neat, tall, conical shape. Its erect sprays of emerald-green foliage will, after about twenty years, attain a height of 10ft and a spread of 3ft, making it an ideal subject for a high hedge. If being grown as a hedge, the individual plants should be set 2ft apart. It only grows at a rate of 9in per year, but may eventually reach a height of 20ft after about fifty years.

It is a solid, reliable performer that will prosper in any reasonably drained, moisture-retentive soil, so add plenty of leaf mould or rotted garden compost when planting and water regularly in hot, dry weather until it is established. It prefers a fairly sunny location but will grow equally well in dappled shade. The tight growing habit means that the only pruning required is to even up the tops if you are growing a hedge. Another good variety for hedging or simply for growing as an individual architectural feature is *T. occidentalis* **'Golden Globe'**, which has attractive yellow-green foliage and naturally forms a more rounded shape 5ft high and wide. Unlike some yellow-leaved conifers, it does not scorch in full sun but needs to be kept watered in hot, dry weather until it is established. It produces reddish-brown cones in autumn.

Likes Any reasonably drained soil in sun or partial shade.
Key points Neat habit, good hedging specimen. Evergreen, long-lived.
VFM 8

PART VII

Shrubs

Shrubs add shape, structure and height to the garden, as well as providing a home and food source for wildlife. Some shrubs are grown for their flowers but others have berries, foliage or stems that are brightly coloured, while evergreen species guarantee year-round interest. Apart from bush roses (which are included in this section), shrubs generally require little attention, although some deciduous species do benefit from annual pruning. Unless stated otherwise, add rotted organic matter or fertiliser to the soil before planting and apply a mulch around the base of the shrub each spring.

As a rule, however, they are low maintenance and many are virtually indestructible. You really don't need green fingers to be successful with the varieties listed here. While shrubs may initially be more expensive than herbaceous perennials, because they can live for thirty years or more they represent very good value for money.

Aucuba japonica (Japanese Laurel)

Grown for its large, glossy, dark-green leaves with striking gold splashes, Japanese laurel is an evergreen shrub that will succeed where many others fail. It grows in any soil that does not become waterlogged and is equally happy exposed to some sun or in deep shade in a woodland setting. In particular, it is one of the few plants that will grow in dry shade and is therefore ideal for planting under trees. It also copes with pollution and salt-laden coastal winds and can be used as an effective hedge. It is completely hardy throughout the UK (to minus 15°C), but as a precaution it might be wise to plant it in a fairly sheltered spot in the coldest areas of the Scottish Highlands.

There are male and female plants. The female forms produce a crop of showy red berries in autumn, but only if cross-pollinated by the rather insignificant, small, purplish flowers found on the male in spring. So to get berries, you need to grow both male and female plants nearby – and for a bumper crop of berries it is recommended that you plant three females to one male. Online retailers should state the sex of each cultivar, but if you are buying at a garden centre and the plants are not clearly labelled, ask an assistant for advice. *A. japonica* **'Crotonifolia'** and *A. japonica* **'Variegata'** are good female forms and *A. japonica* **'Golden King'** and *A. japonica* **'Mr Goldstrike'** are reliable males. To confuse matters further, *A. japonica* **'Rozannie'**, which has plain green leaves, is bisexual, although it still needs a male plant nearby in order to produce berries. Japanese laurel will reach a height and spread of 8ft, but can be kept much shorter by pruning back at any time of year. Otherwise, it needs little attention and can live for over a century.

Likes Any soil in partial or full shade.
Flowering season April–May.
Key points Variegated, evergreen foliage for year-round interest, large red berries in autumn. Will grow in deep shade, long-lived.
VFM 7

Berberis (Barberry)

When it comes to searching for easy-to-grow, low-maintenance shrubs that offer outstanding year-round interest, the 450-strong berberis genus is indispensable. It contains both evergreen and deciduous species. The evergreens produce fabulous floral displays of orange or yellow in spring or early summer, followed in autumn by masses of inky-blue berries that are irresistible to blackbirds; the deciduous forms offer stunning foliage in dark red, pink or gold, along with creamy-yellow flowers and vivid red berries.

Berberises need no attention except for the occasional light trim to keep them in shape, and will grow in any soil and in any location where they receive plenty of sun. There are species ranging from neat rockery dwarfs to 12ft giants; they can be used as individual specimens or to make a formidable hedge. If you are looking for shrubs to form a boundary that will prove impenetrable to intruders, berberises are just the job. A would-be burglar would need a suit of armour to brave the sharp, holly-like leaves of the evergreens and the vicious barbed stems of the deciduous varieties. These same traits also make the larger, bushier types a popular choice for small nesting birds, as larger predators will think twice about entering. What berberises lack in hospitality, however, they more than repay in terms of versatility. These are some of the finest species to seek out:

B. darwinii has everything you could ask for in a shrub. In April and May the entire bush is smothered with clusters of orange-yellow flowers that are tinged with red like a blood orange. These are set against beautiful, dark-green, evergreen leaves that are borne on sturdy, arching branches and are like a smaller version of holly – and every bit as prickly. There is sometimes a second flush of flowers in the autumn, but that season is chiefly reserved for the masses of inky-blue berries. It is a vigorous grower and will reach a height and spread of at least 10ft, so give it room to express itself.

B. linearifolia **'Orange King'** is a fast-growing evergreen shrub that is covered in almost fluorescent orange-yellow flowers in March and April. It has glossy, dark-green leaves and produces purple fruit in autumn. It is a good alternative to *B. darwinii* if space is limited because it has a more upright habit and will only reach a height of 6ft with a spread of 5ft.

B. stenophylla is a spiny, evergreen shrub with narrow, green leaves and carries clusters of bright-yellow flowers along its arching branches in April and May, followed by blue-black berries in autumn. It can eventually reach a height and spread of 12ft, but if trimmed back immediately after flowering it makes an excellent hedge (planted 18in apart). For a rock garden try *B. stenophylla* **'Corallina Compacta'**, which only reaches a height and spread of 18in.

B. thunbergii f. atropurpurea is a deciduous shrub grown princi-pally for its dark-red-purple leaves that turn a more vibrant red in autumn. The foliage is complemented by red-tinged, creamy-yellow flowers in April and May and by glossy red berries in autumn. The young, thorny stems are also a dramatic shade of red. A vigorous grower, it creates a dense bush with a height and spread of 5ft. *B. thunbergii f. atropurpurea* **'Helmond Pillar'** is an upright form (height 5ft, spread 2ft), while *B. thunbergii f. atropurpurea* **'Atropurpurea Nana'** is a dwarf form (height and spread 2ft) suita-ble for large rockeries. For even more dramatic foliage, choose *B. thunbergii* **'Rose Glow'**. In spring, the new shoots are pink and the leaves purple, mottled with pink and white. In April and May it produces small, pale-yellow flowers. As the season progresses, the leaves become increasingly purple and in autumn there is a fine display of red berries. Height and spread 5ft. Another interesting vari-ety is *B. thunbergii f. atropurpurea* **'Golden Ring'**, which has purple leaves edged with yellow, along with pale-yellow flowers followed by crimson berries. As a contrast to the purple-leaved barberries, *B. thunbergii* **'Aurea'** has bright-yellow leaves which turn pale green by early autumn. Red-tinged yellow flowers in April and May are followed by red berries in autumn. Height and spread 5ft. A dwarf form, *B. thunbergii* **'Aurea Nana'**, grows to a height and spread of 2ft.

B. wilsoniae is thorny even by berberis standards. A dense, semi-evergreen, mound-forming bush with arching branches, it has pale-yellow flowers in June and July and small, grey-green leaves. In autumn, the leaves turn red and orange and are joined by clusters of coral-pink berries. Height 3ft, spread 5ft.

Likes Any reasonable soil in sun or light shade.
Flowering season Varies according to species.
Key points Tough, low maintenance, with wonderful floral and foliage displays. Autumn berries are irresistible to birds.
VFM 10

Buddleia davidii (Butterfly Bush)

One look at a buddleia in bloom on a warm summer's day will immediately tell you how it acquired its popular name. The long, tapering, fragrant flower heads in colours ranging from white to deep purple that are borne in clusters at the end of the arching stems are real butterfly magnets, and it is not uncommon to see four or more perched on the same bloom simultaneously. If you are looking to attract wildlife to your garden, a butterfly bush is a must-have shrub. It helps that it is incredibly easy to grow. You only need to travel by train and see how it has colonised swathes of trackside to realise that it is not fussy about growing conditions. It likes full sun and reasonably drained soil, but beyond that it has no special requirements.

It is a deciduous shrub with large, lance-shaped, grey-green leaves that turn yellow in autumn and flowers that can be more than 1ft long. Growth is rapid, and the bush will reach a height of 10ft and a spread of 15ft unless pruned annually. In April each stem should be cut back hard to a strong, low side shoot, effectively removing all of the previous year's growth. This will not only restrict its spread but will encourage a much better display of flowers. Also, after flowering, deadhead by cutting the spent blooms back to a pair of side shoots. This will prevent self-seeding and produce a second flush of flowers. Popular cultivars include **'Black Knight'** (deep purple), **'Charming'** (lavender-pink), **'Empire Blue'** (violet-blue with an orange eye), **'Fortune'** (lilac with an orange eye), **'Nanho Purple'** (purple with an orange eye and only grows to 6ft x 6ft), **'Royal Red'** (wine-red with flowers up to 20in long) and **'White Profusion'** (white). Look out, too, for the hybrid *B.* **'Lochinch'**, which is similar to *B. davidii* but is slightly more compact (height 7ft, spread 10ft) than the bigger forms and has long, lavender-blue spikes that are equally irresistible to butterflies. A series of dwarf varieties of *B. davidii* has been introduced recently, which are ideal for a small garden or even for growing in containers. These only reach a height and spread of around 4ft but are extremely free flowering. Varieties include **'Blue Chip'** (purple), **'Candy Pink'** (pink), **'Indigo'** (dark blue), **'Ivory'** (white) and **'Magenta'** (deep pink).

Likes Reasonably drained soil in full sun.

Flowering season July–September.

Key points Long, elegant, fragrant flower heads, adored by butterflies. Easy to grow.

VFM 8

Chaenomeles (Flowering Quince)

As the name implies, flowering quince is grown for its attractive spring flowers in red, pink or white and its large crop of autumn fruits. These are green ripening to yellow, and when cooked can be used in preserves or jellies (the word 'marmalade' comes from the Portuguese for quince, *marmelo*). The general consensus of opinion is that you should definitely refrain from eating the fruits raw as they have a taste politely described as bitter.

A deciduous shrub with flowers that arrive either before or as the ovate, glossy, dark-green leaves emerge, it naturally grows wider than it does tall and its habit makes it a good plant for training up a wall or for use as a hedge, where its spiny stems create an effective security barrier. If being grown against a wall, it should be pruned back to two or three leaves immediately after flowering to encourage fresh growth. If the shrub is being grown in the open, just trim back lightly after flowering and remove any unwanted stems. Otherwise it needs little attention and will grow in any soil with decent drainage. It prefers a sunny spot but will tolerate some shade. There are also a few double-flowered cultivars, but these will not produce fruit. Even those with semi-double flowers do not fruit as freely as the singles. There are three main species of chaenomeles:

C. japonica – the Japanese quince – produces single, orange-red, cupped flowers for weeks on end. Height 4ft, spread 6ft.

C. speciosa is slightly larger and can reach up to 10ft in height as a wall shrub. *C. speciosa* **'Cardinalis'** has single, scarlet flowers. Height 5ft, spread 7ft. *C. speciosa* **'Geisha Girl'** produces lovely, semi-double, salmon-pink flowers. Height 5ft, spread 5ft. *C. speciosa* **'Moerloosei'** has clusters of pretty, single, soft-pink and white flowers. Height 8ft, spread 15ft. *C. speciosa* **'Nivalis'** has single, pure-white flowers. Height 8ft, spread 15ft. A new variety, *C. speciosa* **'Orange Storm'**, has large, 2in-wide, double, scarlet-red flowers carried on thornless stems. It is a bushier variety but does not produce fruit. Height 4ft, spread 4ft. There is also a pink version,

C. speciosa **'Pink Storm'**. *C. speciosa* **'Simonii'** is a shorter cultivar, with semi-double, blood-red flowers. Height 3ft, spread 5ft.

C. superba is a cross between *C. japonica* and *C. speciosa*. *C. superba* **'Crimson and Gold'** has masses of single, crimson-red flowers with golden anthers on a compact bush (height 3ft, spread 6ft). *C. superba* **'Pink Lady'** has single, rose-pink flowers emerging from deeper pink buds. Height 5ft, spread 6ft.

Likes Any adequately drained soil in sun or partial shade.
Flowering season March–May.
Key points Pretty spring flowers followed in autumn by fruits that can be used in preserves. Good for training up a wall or as a hedge.
VFM 8

Cornus (Dogwood)

Dogwood is a deciduous shrub grown almost exclusively for its spectacular winter and early spring display when its tall, upright, young stems turn a dazzling coral-red or orange, illuminating the garden, especially against a snowy backdrop. To achieve the best colour, the stems should be cut back to within a few inches of the ground in late March or early April, just as the new shoots are emerging, although this will mean sacrificing that year's flowers. These appear in the form of flat-headed, creamy-white clusters in late spring or early summer, but are relatively insignificant compared to the stems. If you do allow your dogwood to produce flowers, they will be followed by groups of blue-tinged, white berries. You can still have flowers, berries *and* beautiful winter stems by choosing to cut back only about a half of the bush each year, but it will eventually become straggly and the display will not be as striking.

Dogwoods are happy in sun or partial shade and thrive in pretty much any soil, notably heavy, wet clay. A spring mulch of rotted compost or manure will boost growth. If you have the space they are at their most effective in groups of three or four, particularly if you mix the red- and orange-stemmed varieties.

C. alba **'Aurea'** has golden-yellow leaves in summer, which intensify in colour in autumn before falling to reveal bright red stems. *C. alba* **'Elegantissima'** has attractive, grey-green leaves with white margins. These turn reddish-orange in autumn and are followed by red stems. *C. alba* **'Sibirica'** – Siberian dogwood – has oval, dark-green leaves, turning red in autumn. The winter stem display is vivid red. For a better summer show try *C. alba* **'Sibirica Variegata'**, which has bright-green leaves with cream margins that are suffused with pink in autumn. In winter, the stems turn bright red. Another outstanding variegated dogwood is *C. alba* **'Spaethii'**, whose yellow-margined, green leaves turn plum-purple in autumn before dropping to show off mahogany-red stems. Each of these cultivars can reach a height and spread of 10ft.

C. sanguinea **'Midwinter Fire'** bears mid-green leaves that turn orange-yellow in autumn. The winter stems are yellow at the base, rising to fiery, orange-red at the top, like a bush fire. A more compact form than *C. alba*, it will reach a height and spread of 5ft.

Likes Any soil – even wet ground – in sun or partial shade.
Flowering season May–June.
Key points Dramatic red or orange stems in winter and early spring, autumn foliage colour. Some have variegated or golden leaves in summer. Creamy-white flowers, blue-white berries.
VFM 9

Cotinus coggygria (Smoke Bush)

Every garden needs shrubs with stunning foliage, and if you have the space there are few that give a more dramatic display than the smoke bush. Its substantial framework is covered with large, rounded, purple leaves on red stems during summer; in autumn the foliage turns a brilliant scarlet, looking sensational when backlit by the September sun. Its name comes from the feathery, plume-like, pinkish-purple flower heads, which resemble a haze of smoke.

It is an easy shrub to grow, flourishing in any soil. When planting, add leaf mould but not manure or too much rotted compost because the autumn leaf colour is not as impressive when the soil is rich. Similarly, although it will grow in some shade, the best results are achieved in a sunny location. In March, the smoke bush should be cut back hard and any dead wood removed to keep it compact and encourage larger leaves. Excellent red varieties include *C. coggygria* **'Royal Purple'** (height and spread 12ft) and the hybrid, *C.* **'Grace'**, which is a particularly vigorous grower, reaching a height of 20ft and a spread of 15ft. *C. coggygria* **'Flame'** (height 20ft, spread 15ft) has light-green leaves that turn a magnificent orange-red in autumn.

Likes Any soil in sun or light shade.
Flowering season July–September.
Key points Beautiful purple and scarlet foliage in summer and autumn. Easy to grow.
VFM 8

Cotoneaster

Cotoneasters are versatile shrubs, offering everything from low-growing groundcover to high hedges. Their small, glossy green leaves and inconspicuous flowers in summer are followed by masses of red autumn berries that last well into winter – if they have not been devoured by foraging birds. These shrubs may not be the showiest of performers but they are easy going, reliable and tough, and the only pruning they require is the occasional trim to maintain shape. They are unconcerned about soil type so long as the drainage is reasonable, and will grow in sun or partial shade.

It is a large genus, but these are some of the more notable varieties:

C. atropurpureus **'Variegatus'** is a dense, spreading, groundcover shrub with stiff branches and oval-shaped deciduous leaves that are mid-green with white edges and turn pink and red in autumn before they fall. In May it bears small, pink flowers, followed in autumn and winter by plenty of red berries. A good plant for scrambling down a bank or low wall. Height 18in, spread 3ft.

C. conspicuus **'Decorus'** is a mound-forming, evergreen shrub with glossy green, oval-shaped leaves. It produces a profusion of small white flowers in May, followed by a long display of red berries. Height 5ft, spread 7ft.

C. horizontalis is a spreading, deciduous shrub with flat branches that form a herringbone pattern, and glossy green leaves that turn red in autumn. It has tiny pinkish-white flowers in May, followed by bright-red berries. This is a useful plant for training up a north- or east-facing wall. Height 3ft, spread 5ft. There is also a variegated form, *C. horizontalis* **'Variegatus'**, with white-margined leaves that turn pink and red in autumn. It is less vigorous than *C. horizontalis*, reaching a height of only 18in and a spread of 3ft.

C. lacteus is a tall, evergreen shrub which, if pruned into shape in spring, can make an excellent hedge. Its arching branches bear clusters of white flowers in June and July and attractive, olive-green leaves which have distinctive, grey, woolly undersides. In autumn it produces an abundance of red berries that can last until January. Height and spread 10ft.

C. simonsii is an upright, deciduous or semi-evergreen form with shiny green leaves that redden into autumn. It produces bee-friendly, white flowers in June and July and then bright orange-red berries in autumn and winter. This is another species that can make a good hedge. Height 10ft, spread 6ft.

C. suecicus **'Coral Beauty'** is a low-growing, spreading evergreen that has glossy green leaves and is smothered from May to June in white flowers. These are followed in autumn by an abundance of red berries. Height 3ft, spread 6ft.

Likes Any reasonably drained soil in sun or partial shade.

Flowering season May–July.

Key points Glossy green leaves and colourful autumn berries that birds love. Many species are evergreen for winter interest. Low maintenance.

VFM 7

Crataegus (Hawthorn)

Some gardeners might balk at the idea of growing hawthorn, but not only does the common species form a highly effective, impenetrable hedge much loved by wildlife, there are also a couple of other hawthorns that make admirable, free-standing, deciduous shrubs or trees. Hawthorn grows in any soil and is incredibly tough, able to withstand everything the UK climate throws at it, from storms and gales to drought. It is a plant for any region, coping with city pollution and salty coastal air alike. It only needs pruning if you want to keep it as a relatively neat hedge – otherwise just let it grow naturally and you will be rewarded for fifty years or more with an abundance of sweetly scented flowers followed by autumn berries.

C. laevigata **'Paul's Scarlet'** is a tall hawthorn (height and spread 25ft) that produces lobed, glossy green leaves and clusters of double, dark-pink flowers followed in autumn by small red berries. *C. laevigata* **'Rosea Flore Pleno'** has paler pink, double flowers.

C. lavallei **'Carrierei'** is a vigorous hawthorn that in late spring bears pretty, single, white flowers with a red centre. These are followed by small orange-red haws, which ripen in autumn and last well into winter. The flowers and berries are shaded by the shiny green leaves, which turn shades of orange and red in autumn and are one of the last deciduous trees to drop. Even the bark is an attractive silvery grey. Height and spread 30ft.

C. monogyna – the common hawthorn or may – is a rounded tree with glossy leaves and white flowers, followed in autumn by dark-red berries. It can reach an eventual height and spread of 25ft, but can also be trained as a hedge. The small saplings should be set about 14in apart; once the hedge is established, it can be trimmed to shape in June.

Likes Any soil in sun or partial shade.

Flowering season March–May.

Key points Tough, easy to grow, low maintenance. Flowers and berries, a natural haven for wildlife. Long-lived.

VFM 7

Escallonia

Gardening books and websites often list escallonia as a tender shrub, suitable only for coastal gardens or sheltered spots, but it is much more hardy than people realise. I have grown two in my garden in Nottingham – one in a particularly exposed spot – for years without experiencing any problems. Native to South America, escallonia can withstand temperatures as low as minus 15°C, and is therefore able to withstand our severest winters. Nevertheless – to be on the safe side – if you live in the far north of the UK it is probably advisable to plant it in a fairly sheltered spot against a south- or west-facing fence or wall, and certainly away from cold winds. It is a shrub that is well worth accommodating because it forms a dense, evergreen bush that is absolutely smothered with pink or crimson flowers in mid-summer. Set off perfectly by the shiny green leaves, these flowers appear to attract bees from miles around, and it is not unusual to have dozens of insects feeding on the blossom simultaneously. On a sunny day, the entire bush seems to buzz.

It will grow in any fertile soil – add plenty of compost or fertiliser before planting – and it does like a sunny position. Pruning is optional, but if you want to keep it in shape (for instance, if you are growing it as a hedge), give the branches a light trim in late summer after flowering. These are some of the most reliable varieties:

E. **'Apple Blossom'** bears masses of delightful, tubular flowers that are clear pink with a white base – just like . . . apple blossom. It is slower growing than some escallonias and will reach a height and spread of 8ft.

E. **'Donard Radiance'** has pretty, fragrant, crimson-red flowers. Height and spread 5ft.

E. **'Donard Seedling'** is a vigorous shrub whose arching branches can quickly reach a height and spread of 9ft. The flowers are white, suffused pink, emerging from pink buds, and are pleasantly scented.

E. **'Red Dream'** is a more compact cultivar, growing to 2ft high and 3ft wide, with crimson-red flowers and lush foliage.

E. rubra var. macrantha **'Crimson Spire'** is one of the toughest escallonias, eventually reaching a height and spread of 12ft. It has crimson-red flowers and shiny green leaves.

Likes Reasonably drained soil in full sun.
Flowering season May–July.
Key points Evergreen shrub smothered in glossy leaves and pretty, fragrant flowers. Attracts bees.
VFM 8

Euonymus fortunei (Spindle)

This is a very useful evergreen for providing variegated foliage all year round. A versatile performer, it can be used as groundcover, as a stand-alone bush or for climbing up a fence. Indeed, if you do plant it anywhere near a fence or wall, its natural instinct seems to be to scramble up it, to a height of 15ft or more. It thrives in any soil that does not become completely waterlogged, and although the leaf colour is generally best in full sun, it will still put on a fine show in light shade. Once established, it needs no attention but will not resent the occasional light trim to prevent it suffocating more delicate plants in the vicinity. Despite being grown for its foliage, it does have small, pale-green flowers in early summer, occasionally followed by fruits. Here are some cultivars to look out for:

E. fortunei **'Emerald Gaiety'** is an elegant variety bearing glossy, emerald-green leaves with snowy white margins that become flushed with pink in winter. It has insignificant, green flowers in May. Height 3ft, spread 5ft.

E. fortunei **'Emerald 'n' Gold'** is a popular, low-growing, spreading shrub with shiny green leaves that have broad, golden-yellow margins. From a distance, the whole plant looks yellow, making it an ideal specimen for scrambling up a dark fence. The leaves are tinged with pink in very cold weather and it sometimes produces green flowers in early summer. It grows to a height of 2ft and a spread of 3ft, but if trained up a wall can reach 15ft.

E. fortunei **'Harlequin'** has leaves which change colour with the seasons. The young spring foliage is pure white but then it becomes mottled with shades of green, eventually developing a pink tinge in winter. Height 2ft, spread 3ft.

E. fortunei **'Silver Queen'** is a larger, more upright shrub than the others. The leaves are dark green with broad, creamy margins that become tinged with pink during frosty weather. It has greenish-white flowers and occasional pale pink fruits. Height 8ft, spread 5ft.

Likes Any soil in full sun or light shade.

Flowering season May–June.

Key points Attractive variegated, evergreen leaves give year-round interest. Easy to grow, extremely low maintenance. Can be used as a climber.

VFM 8

Forsythia intermedia

Spring is a golden time in the garden, and not just because of daffodils. For many a shrubbery or hedge is illuminated by the forsythia, a vigorous, deciduous shrub. Tubular, bright-yellow flowers cover every inch of its bare branches. It is a real sunshine yellow – full on and in your face – and the sheer profusion of flowers so early in the gardening season amply compensates for any lack of subtlety.

The mid-green, oval leaves emerge after flowering on branches that can eventually reach a height and spread of 10ft if left unchecked – and be warned, forsythia can quickly develop into an ungainly sprawl. Should you need to keep it to a more modest size (almost certainly the case if you plan to grow several as an informal hedge), cut back the stems that have just flowered on established plants by at least a third to a pair of strong buds immediately after the blooms have finished. Additionally, once the plant is five or six years old, cut back a couple of the old stems to within a few inches of the ground in order to promote the growth of new basal shoots. Timing is all-important: if you prune too late in the year, you will be cutting off next year's flowering growth as it is a shrub that blooms on stems and buds made in the previous year. Forsythias are tough cookies, happy in any reasonably drained soil and prospering either in full sun or partial shade. Add plenty of rotted garden compost or farmyard manure when planting. *F. intermedia* is the most popular garden species, **'Lynwood Variety'** and **'Spectabilis'** being among the most reliable cultivars. The latter also has a variegated form, *F. intermedia* **'Spectabilis Variegata'**, with green and yellow leaves through summer as a change from the usual green.

Likes Reasonably drained, fertile soil in full sun or partial shade.
Flowering season February–April.
Key points Dazzling display of yellow flowers in early spring. Can be used as an informal hedge.
VFM 8

Hypericum (St John's Wort)

It is easy to dismiss hypericum as something of a second-rate shrub that has a habit of self-seeding where you least want it to, but while it may not be in the same class as, for example, rhododendrons or camellias, it does possess a number of virtues. It will grow in any soil in any position where it receives some sun, its buttercup-yellow flowers are borne in considerable numbers over a long period well into autumn when few shrubs remain in bloom, it does not grow to an unmanageable size, and requires no serious pruning. Just give it an annual trim in spring, removing any straggly stems that spoil the overall shape of the bush. It is semi-evergreen, the oval-shaped leaves sometimes remaining through mild winters, and some species have the bonus of autumn fruits. The common St John's wort – *hypericum perforatum* – has been used medicinally since the days of Hippocrates and often features in modern herbal remedies to treat depression and insomnia. As well as the larger shrubs, which can reach a height of 5ft, there are dwarf forms suitable as groundcover or for a rock garden.

H. calycinum – Rose of Sharon – is a good groundcover plant, especially for a difficult, dry, semi-shaded spot under trees, but avoid planting it too near any choice specimens because it will quickly overwhelm them. It grows to a height of 18in but spreads by runners to cover an area of 6 sq ft or more. Keep it in check by cutting the stems back to the ground in spring before new growth appears. The large, yellow flowers have prominent, red-tipped anthers and are carried for months against dark-green leaves.

H. hidcoteense **'Hidcote'** is a popular cultivar that produces masses of large, 3in-wide, saucer-shaped, yellow flowers with orange anthers on reddish stems over a long period. It reaches a height and spread of 5ft and, if planted in groups, can be used as an informal hedge. It rarely produces fruit.

H. inodorum **'Elstead'** produces clusters of 1in-wide, star-shaped, yellow flowers, followed by showy, orange-red fruits. Height and spread 4ft.

H. moserianum **'Tricolor'** is a dwarf cultivar with yellow flowers and variegated leaves that are green edged with pink and white. Height 1ft, spread 2ft.

H. **'Orange Flair'** is a new, free-flowering, compact hypericum with yellow flowers and orange-red berries. Height and spread 2ft 6in.

H. perforatum is a more upright shrub (height 3ft, spread 18in) with star-shaped, yellow flowers that are sometimes tinged with red (smaller than those on *H. hidcoteense* **'Hidcote'**). *H. perforatum* occasionally produces fruit.

Likes Any reasonably drained soil in full sun or partial shade.
Flowering season July–October.
Key points Long flowering season, unfussy, low maintenance, self-seeds to provide extra plants. Some species have attractive, orange-red, berry-like fruits.
VFM 8

Ilex (Holly)

Holly is one of our most recognisable shrubs, as synonymous with Christmas as robins and mince pies. However (in this case at least), familiarity should not be allowed to breed contempt because holly can have a valuable role to play in the garden, both as a stalwart of the shrubbery and as an impenetrable hedge. Obviously the brilliant red berries are the chief attraction, but, like Japanese laurel, these only appear on the female plants, so you will need to grow a male holly nearby to enjoy the fruits of your labour.

But the appeal of holly is by no means confined to its berries. Choose an evergreen species with variegated foliage and you will be able to admire glossy, green-and-yellow or green-and-cream leaves all year round. If you are worried about the thorns, there are even cultivars that are virtually spineless. Holly also bears small white flowers in late spring. It will grow in any reasonably fertile soil with decent drainage (add some rotted compost or manure when planting) and, although it tolerates light shade, it produces a better crop of fruit in full sun. Plants grown as free-standing shrubs require minimal pruning – just an occasional light trim to keep a good shape – but those being grown as formal hedges should be trimmed to shape in late summer. After pruning, apply a mulch of compost around the base of the plant. Here are some hollies that are worth searching out:

I. altaclerensis **'Golden King'** (female) has beautiful, variegated leaves with dark-green centres and creamy-yellow margins. It produces small white flowers in May, followed by reddish-brown berries in autumn that ripen to red. Height 20ft, spread 15ft. For a hedge, plant 18in apart. *I. altaclerensis* **'Lawsoniana'** (female) bears large, usually spineless, green leaves that are splashed with gold. White spring flowers are succeeded by red berries in autumn and winter. Height 20ft, spread 15ft.

I. aquifolium – the English holly – is a tall, slow-growing, bushy shrub with purple stems, creamy flowers, glossy foliage and, when planted near a male, a good crop of red berries. *I. aquifolium* **'Golden**

Milkboy' (male) has spiny, dark-green leaves with a huge, central golden blotch. Being male, it produces no berries. Height 20ft, spread 12ft. *I. aquifolium* **'Handsworth New Silver'** (female) has purple stems and long, spiny, grey-green leaves edged in cream. Free fruiting. Height 25ft, spread 15ft. *I. aquifolium* **'J. C. van Tol'** is a self-pollinating female, so unusually does not need to be planted near a male holly in order to produce red berries. Its leaves are plain green and almost thornless. Height 20ft, spread 12ft. *I. aquifolium* **'Madame Briot'** (female) has spiny, dark-green leaves that are blotched and margined with golden yellow, the leaves contrasting nicely with the purple stems. Red berries. Height 30ft, spread 15ft. *I. aquifolium* **'Silver Queen'** (male) has spiny, dark-green leaves with creamy-white edges. No berries. Height 30ft, spread 12ft.

I. crenata **'Golden Gem'** is a low-growing, spreading, evergreen shrub with spineless, golden-yellow leaves. It is a good holly for a small garden, but the downside is that it does not produce its white flowers and black berries in great numbers. Height 4ft, spread 5ft.

I. meserveae **'Blue Angel = Conang'** (female) is a dense, slow-growing evergreen with purplish stems and spiny, glossy blue-green leaves. The small pinkish-white flowers are followed by red berries. Height 10ft, spread 8ft. *I. meserveae* **'Blue Prince = Conablu'** (male) has pinkish-white, late spring flowers and spiny, shiny blue-green foliage. No berries. Height 10ft, spread 8ft.

Likes Any reasonably drained soil in sun or light shade.
Flowering season April–June.
Key points Evergreen foliage (often variegated) for year-round interest and bright-red winter berries that attract birds. Good, impenetrable hedging plant.
VFM 8

Kerria japonica 'Pleniflora' (Bachelor's Buttons)

Compared to annuals and hardy perennials, the majority of shrubs have a relatively short flowering season, relying instead on their stems or foliage to provide a longer period of interest. But this is a shrub that can be in bloom virtually all year round. During spring its tall green canes are smothered in large, double, orange-yellow pompoms, but even after the main flowering period is over it keeps on producing a handful of blooms, sometimes right through winter. It just never knows when to have a rest.

It will grow almost anywhere, but is best planted in a position that receives some shade because full sun may bleach the blooms. It is ideal for brightening up a dull corner or a north- or east-facing wall, its jolly flowers surrounded by deciduous light-green leaves with serrated edges. A vigorous shrub, it can reach a height of 8ft and will spread to 10ft or more by means of suckers growing from its creeping roots. New shoots rise up from the base each year and, if space is not a problem, you can simply leave it be and limit pruning to the removal of any dead wood. However, if you wish to restrict its influence, cut the canes back hard at the end of May (after the principal flowering season), pruning some stems right down to the ground. This may seem drastic, but it will help to rejuvenate the kerria and ensure even better blooms for years to come.

Likes Any reasonably drained soil in partial shade.
Flowering season March–May.
Key points Repeat flowers over a long period, easy to grow, low maintenance.
VFM 9

Lonicera purpusii 'Winter Beauty' (Winter Honeysuckle)

Winter fragrance is hard to find in the garden, but one plant that has it in spades is the winter honeysuckle. Unlike its trickier summer cousin, it is not a climber but a stand-alone shrub: a vigorous grower that will rapidly reach a height of 6ft and a spread of 8ft. It is deciduous, and in the coldest months of the year its bare branches are smothered in small, tubular white flowers with prominent yellow anthers that emit the most wonderful citrus-lemon fragrance. The scent is so powerful in the chill air that it can be detected from several yards away. The flowers first appear in December and last right through until late March, providing prolonged colour at what can otherwise be a fairly barren time of year.

Winter honeysuckle races away in any reasonable soil and in any position where it receives some sun. If you want to control its spread, prune established plants in April after flowering, cutting back the stems that have just flowered by about a third. If it has really outgrown its space you can be more brutal, hacking it right back to strong buds close to the ground. Don't worry: it will quickly recover. You might not get too many flowers the following winter, but it will soon be filling the air again with its heady scent and will continue to do so for many years to come.

The only negative to winter honeysuckle is that, once it has finished flowering, it has little to offer. The leaves are nothing out of the ordinary and it just tends to sit there occupying a lot of space. Therefore either mix it with summer-flowering shrubs or try growing climbing plants up it – a clematis or two or a small climbing rose – to provide some summer colour for the area. Plant the climber on the outside of the honeysuckle and in a hole wide enough so that you can slightly angle it towards the shrub and there are branches for support. The only thing you need to watch out for is that the honeysuckle leaves don't obscure the climber's flowers, so remove any foliage that threatens to spoil the display. *Lonicera fragrantissima* is the basic winter honeysuckle, but *L. purpusii* **'Winter Beauty'** is considered to be even better. Plant it alongside a path where you can enjoy its delicious scent all through winter.

Likes Any reasonably drained soil in sun or partial shade.
Flowering season December–March.
Key points Fabulous lemon fragrance, winter interest. Long flowering season, easy to grow.
VFM 9

Mahonia japonica

The mahonia is an under-rated evergreen, possibly because one of the most common forms, the compact, spring-flowering *M. aquifolium*, is something of a poor man's berberis. Its clusters of golden-yellow flowers are nothing remarkable, and, although it goes on to produce black berries, its tendency to spread by means of suckers can give the impression that it is more of a weed to be tolerated than a magnificent shrub in its own right. However, two other mahonias – *M. japonica* and its hybrid, *M. media* – are more than a match for berberises. Not only do they produce long, elegant racemes of soft yellow flowers followed by blue-black berries, those flowers have a sweet, lily-of-the-valley fragrance that is much loved by bees. They bloom throughout winter on stems carrying glossy, dark-green leaves which, although spiny, are not as potent as those on a berberis. The other thing that mahonias have going for them is that they thrive in a shaded spot – indeed, full sun can scorch their leaves, so they prefer to be planted out of direct sunlight. They like moist soil with decent drainage (not waterlogged), and need no real pruning other than the removal of any dead wood after flowering.

M. japonica is a beautiful shrub with highly fragrant, lemon-yellow flowers that are carried in drooping sprays from late autumn right through to spring, when it produces dark-blue berries that are a valuable source of food for nest-building birds. The shiny green leaves are flushed with red in extreme cold. It is a good plant for a woodland border, provided you plant it close to a path where you can appreciate its heady scent. It is not a fast grower, but after twenty years you can expect it to reach a height of about 6ft and a spread of around 8ft.

M. media is a hybrid of *M. japonica* and *M. lomariifolia* and is suitable for larger gardens as it can eventually grow to a height of 16ft with a 12ft spread. It, too, has fragrant, lemon-yellow flowers on racemes that can be up to 18in long (and are therefore prized for flower arrangements), followed by blue-black berries. If it becomes too leggy, cut it back by a third after flowering to encourage new growth from lower down the bush. Useful cultivars include *M. media* **'Buckland'**, *M. media* **'Charity'**, *M. media* **'Lionel Fortescue'** and *M. media* **'Winter Sun'**.

Likes Moisture-retentive soil in partial or deep shade.
Flowering season November–March.
Key points Soft yellow flowers have wonderful lily-of-the-valley fragrance. Long flowering season, evergreen with blue-black berries, birds and bees attracted to berries and flowers respectively. Winter interest, low maintenance.
VFM 10

Philadelphus (Mock Orange)

Philadelphus is a genus of deciduous shrubs known for their enchantingly fragrant white flowers, both in single and double forms. It is commonly known as 'Mock Orange' because the flowers resemble those of orange blossom. The scent, which has delicious overtones of vanilla, lures bees from all over the neighbourhood and is at its best on warm summer evenings when it wafts across the garden. An undemanding shrub, it can cope with urban pollution and salt air, and is thus equally comfortable in city and coastal gardens. It likes moderately fertile soil (so add some rotted compost or farmyard manure at planting time) and decent drainage, and although it does tolerate some shade it flowers best in full sun.

Immediately after flowering, cut the stems that have just borne flowers right back to strong side shoots and remove any dead wood. With mature bushes, you can also prune a handful (about one in four) of the old stems back to ground level to reinvigorate them for the following year.

There are a number of lovely varieties to choose from, but these are some of the best:

P. **'Beauclerk'** bears clusters of large, fragrant, single, white flowers that are flushed purple at the centre and contrast with the dark-green leaves. Slightly arching in habit. Height and spread 7ft.

P. **'Belle Etoile'** carries a multitude of large, fragrant, single, white flowers with a flush of purple at the centre and bright-yellow stamens. The young stems are a mahogany colour and the leaves are tapered and dark green. Height 4ft, spread 8ft.

P. coronarius **'Aureus'** has fragrant, single, creamy-white flowers and arching branches bearing leaves that are golden-yellow when young before turning yellow-green with age. Height 8ft, spread 5ft. *P. coronarius* **'Variegatus'** is similar, but its mid-green leaves are heavily edged with white. Height 8ft, spread 5ft.

P. **'Manteau d'Hermine'** is a lovely, compact, spreading shrub that produces masses of double, fragrant, creamy-white flowers among mid-green foliage. An excellent specimen for the front of a border. Height 3ft, spread 5ft.

P. **'Snowbelle'** is another compact double whose scented, white flowers are offset by dark-green leaves. Height and spread 4ft.

P. **'Virginal'** has double, fragrant, pure-white flowers among dark-green leaves that turn yellow in autumn. Height 10ft, spread 8ft.

Likes Any reasonably drained soil in full sun or light shade.

Flowering season June–July.

Key points Richly fragrant white flowers on a neat bush. Attracts bees, easy to grow.

VFM 9

Potentilla fruticosa (Shrubby Cinquefoil)

For the front of a shrubbery or a mixed border (or even as a low hedge) you could do a lot worse than try a few shrubby potentillas. They make neat, compact, deciduous bushes with small, green or grey-green leaves and bear a profusion of five-petalled, saucer-shaped flowers in various colours over a long period from late spring through to autumn. The yellows and whites are the most reliably prolific flowerers, but there are also eye-catching pinks, peaches, tangerines and reds (although the blooms of some reds can fade in full sun). Generally, potentillas like sun but will cope with light shade. They like decent drainage and will even do well on poor soil. Many are drought tolerant, but it is a good idea to give them a spring mulch to retain some moisture during the height of summer.

A light trim after flowering will help to keep the bush tidy, and at the same time any tired old wood can be cut back to the base in order to stimulate regrowth. Deadheading the old flowers may encourage new blooms. Here are some cultivars to look out for:

P. fruticosa **'Abbotswood'** has large, white blooms with yellow centres and dark-green leaves that turn auburn in autumn. Height 3ft, spread 4ft.

P. fruticosa **'Daydawn'** has flowers that are a delicate shade of peachy-pink – an unusual but welcome colour for a shrub. Height 3ft, spread 4ft.

P. fruticosa **'Elizabeth'** bears masses of canary-yellow flowers for months on end against a backdrop of dark leaves. Height 3ft, spread 5ft.

P. fruticosa **'Katherine Dykes'** displays more upright growth with grey-green leaves and canary-yellow flowers. Height 4ft, spread 3ft.

P. fruticosa **'Marian Red Robin'** (**'Marrob'**) has dark-green leaves and yellow-centred red flowers that fade to orange in full sun. Plant in light shade to preserve colour. Height and spread 3ft.

P. fruticosa **'Pink Beauty'** carries mid-pink flowers on a tidy mound of grey-green leaves. Height and spread 3ft.

P. fruticosa **'Primrose Beauty'** produces dainty, primrose-yellow flowers with darker eyes against grey-green foliage. Height 3ft, spread 5ft.

P. fruticosa **'Red Ace'** has bright-red flowers with yellow centres, the blooms fading to orange in hot weather. The leaves are grey-green. Plant in light shade if possible for best colour. Height and spread 3ft.

P. fruticosa **'Sunset'** has large, yellow flowers that are flushed with orange and are surrounded by mid-green leaves. Height and spread 3ft.

P. fruticosa **'Tangerine'** has grey-green leaves and orange-yellow flowers. Height and spread 3ft.

P. fruticosa **'White Lady'** produces white flowers with yellow centres above a mound of grey-green foliage. Height and spread 3ft.

Likes Reasonably drained soil in full sun.
Flowering season April–October.
Key points Good range of colours, long flowering season. Neat shrubs, low maintenance.
VFM 8

Prunus cistena (Purple Leaf Sand Cherry)

If you don't have room for a full-blown flowering cherry tree in your garden, there is an alternative: a member of the genus that only reaches a height of about 6ft and a spread of 4ft and boasts beautiful, coloured foliage from spring through to autumn. In spring the branches of the deciduous *Prunus cistena* are adorned with delicate, single, pinkish-white flowers with dark-red stamens. The flowers emerge from pink buds and are soon followed by red leaves, which mature through summer to reddish-purple before changing to greeny-bronze in the autumn. If you're lucky, you may even see some dark fruits.

An accommodating shrub, it thrives in any soil that does not become waterlogged, and while full sun is best for leaf colour, it is also happy in light shade (too much shade and the foliage may revert to green). It even grows well on poor soil and is able to cope both with extreme heat and extreme cold. It can either be grown as a stand-alone shrub or, planted at 1ft intervals, as a hedge. After flowering, cut the stems back to strong new side shoots. This not only controls the shape of the bush (it can become straggly without annual pruning) but will also encourage the growth of more of those young red leaves. If you are training it as a hedge, trim the shoot tips after flowering to encourage it to branch out horizontally as well as vertically. Don't worry if you get it wrong at first; this is also quite a forgiving plant. It may not be one of the longest living of shrubs (its typical lifespan is about fifteen years), but its flowers and foliage make it worth considering for a smaller garden.

Likes Any reasonably drained soil in sun or light shade.
Flowering season March–April.
Key points Pretty pink-cherry flowers set against purple foliage. Makes an attractive hedge.
VFM 7

Pyracantha (Firethorn)

Pyracantha is one of the most adaptable garden shrubs. It can be grown as a stand-alone bush, as a thorny, evergreen hedge that is attractive to nesting birds (but not to vandals), or as a climber, trained up walls so that it can show off its spectacular red, orange or yellow berries in autumn and winter. It is also pretty much a 'grow anywhere' shrub, unfussy about soil or position. It does equally well in dry, free-draining chalk or in any heavy clay that does not get waterlogged, and prospers in sun or shade (although the berry count may be reduced in deep shade). The berries are preceded in late spring by clusters of hawthorn-like, white flowers, which are produced on the previous year's growth.

Pruning is only necessary to restrict height or maintain shape, especially when it is being used as a hedge or climber. Unwanted or damaged growth should be removed in early spring, but on wall-trained pyracanthas new growth can be trimmed in late summer so that the berries do not become obscured by foliage. (For details on creating a framework for climbing plants, see the following section on Climbers.) Overgrown specimens can be cut back hard between spring and late summer. This will encourage them to bush out more. Remember to wear gardening gloves when performing pruning duties because the thorns are not to be messed with. Here are a few of the best cultivars:

P. **'Fiery Cascade'** has small, shiny leaves, white flowers and an abundance of small orange-red berries. Height and spread 9ft.

P. **'Orange Glow'** has glossy, dark-green leaves, white flowers and bright-orange berries. Height and spread 10ft.

P. **'Saphyr Jaune' ('Cadaune')** has dark-green leaves, white flowers and bright-yellow berries. Height and spread 10ft.

P. **'Saphyr Rouge' ('Cadrou')** has white flowers and vivid red berries that eventually turn orange. Height and spread 10ft.

P. **'Soleil d'Or'** has white flowers followed by golden-yellow berries. Height and spread 10ft.

P. **'Watereri'** produces white flowers followed by masses of red fruits. Height and spread 8ft.

Likes Any reasonable soil in sun or shade.
Flowering season May–June.
Key points White flowers in spring followed by beautiful berries in autumn and winter, much loved by blackbirds and thrushes. Can be used as a climber or a hedge. Evergreen, easy to grow.
VFM 8

Ribes sanguineum (Flowering Currant)

The flowering currant is a dependable, medium-sized, deciduous shrub for the spring garden, bearing hanging clusters of red, pink or white flowers in great numbers. The rounded leaves are aromatic and the flowers are followed in summer by blue-black, berry-like fruits. It will succeed in any good garden soil (add rotted compost or manure when planting) and will cope with some shade. It can also be employed as a colourful hedge, which should be trimmed after flowering to retain a neat shape.

Grown as a bush, flowering currants can be left unpruned, but for the best display cut back the branches that have just flowered to strong buds in late summer. These are some good cultivars:

R. sanguineum **'Brocklebankii'** is a slow-growing, compact currant with yellow leaves in spring and pink flowers. It is best planted in semi-shade. Height and spread 4ft.

R. sanguineum **'Elkington's White'** has bright-green leaves and white flowers. Height and spread 6ft.

R. sanguineum **'King Edward VII'** produces mid-green leaves and deep-crimson flowers. Height and spread 5ft.

R. sanguineum **'Koja'** has green leaves and large crimson flowers. Height and spread 5ft.

R. sanguineum **'Pulborough Scarlet'** is a vigorous form with dark-green leaves and magenta-pink flowers with white centres. Very free flowering. Height and spread 8ft.

Likes Any reasonably drained soil in sun or partial shade.
Flowering season March–April.
Key points Spring flowers followed by summer fruits. Easy to grow, can be used as a hedge.
VFM 8

Rosa (Bush Rose)

The rose is unquestionably the nation's favourite flower, and on a summer's day nothing in the garden can compare with the scent of a rose in full bloom. To me, a rose must either have a wonderful colour or a fabulous fragrance – and preferably both. When my father first started growing roses in the 1960s, we grew a French-bred hybrid tea rose named 'Papa Meilland' which had huge, rich, dark velvety-red blooms with a divine fragrance. Sadly, its general health deteriorated and it is not easy to find these days, but it remains the benchmark by which I measure all other rose fragrances, especially reds (on a scale of 1 to 10, with 10 being the best). A red rose is nothing without fragrance.

Roses are such versatile performers. Exquisitely shaped hybrid teas look stately in rose beds, free-flowering floribundas shine when planted in borders with herbaceous perennials, English roses (crosses between hybrid teas, floribundas and old roses) are wonderful for creating a cottage-garden effect among perennials, the larger old roses and shrub roses complement other flowering bushes, rugosa roses make colourful, perfumed hedges, patio roses are great for containers, climbers and ramblers (see Part VIII) add height and structure, and there are even roses for groundcover. It is not only the blooms of a rose that offer colour. Depending on the variety, the young leaf shoots can be purple-red, pale green or coppery-orange and provide a show of their own when glistening in the spring sunshine.

Yet for all its virtues, some gardeners think the rose is too much trouble. Roses could certainly never be described as low maintenance, but they really only need a few hours' attention each year and are actually very easy to grow . . . and keep going for at least ten years.

Planting

As with any garden specimen, planting is the most important time. You can buy roses either as bare-root plants or in pots. A container-grown rose can be planted at any time of year, but bare-root roses, which usually work out cheaper, are delivered in the winter months. You might worry about putting an expensive rose in the ground in December or January, but – provided the soil is not bone hard with frost – roses can be planted throughout winter. They are tougher than you think.

After giving the rose a good soak, choose a site that receives plenty of sun during the day (at least four hours) and dig a hole that is wide and deep enough for the roots to be spread out. Roses love clay, but always add some multi-purpose compost in the bottom of the planting hole so that the roots have an easy passage at first. Also add plenty of well-rotted manure or garden compost to improve the soil. If you are planting where another rose was growing previously, first dig out the soil to a depth of at least 18in and replace it with soil from a different part of the garden as roses can suffer from replant disease. Once you have completed your preparations, place the rose in the centre of the hole so that the graft union at the base of the stems is at ground level. Backfill the hole with more compost and carefully tread down the soil to ensure that the bush is firm and will not rock in strong winds. Treading may press the soil down a little, so don't forget to add more compost to raise it to the required level around the base of the plant. Finally, give it another good watering and continue to water once a day for the next few days unless nature does the job for you.

Pruning

The other principal job is pruning, which should be carried out between February and the end of March (depending on where you live). In Nottingham I usually prune around mid-March, but if you live in the south you can do it earlier. Try not to prune at a time when a sharp frost is forecast. Stems of hybrid teas should be cut back by up to three-quarters, to just above strong side shoots near the base. Floribundas, English roses, miniature and patio roses should be cut back by about a half. Repeat-flowering old roses and shrub roses should be pruned by about a third, but those that produce only a single flush can either be left alone or lightly pruned after flowering. At the same time, remove any dead or weak stems or any stems that cross, as these can cause disease. Always try to select an outward-facing shoot as your cutting point because this will improve the eventual shape of your rose and reduce the risk of stems crossing.

Care

When you prune in spring, sprinkle some proprietary rose food (see details on the box for quantities) around the base of the plant and hoe in lightly. If the weather is dry, give the ground some water. Another feed in early July and a spring mulch will also prove beneficial. Unless you want to encourage your rose to form hips (the colourful seed-pods), deadhead regularly throughout the season. When removing the old flowers, don't be afraid to cut long stems back by a foot or more to a strong side shoot to keep the bush looking shapely. Good care of your rose should also help to reduce the risk of diseases such as black spot and mildew, while greenfly can either be removed by hand or with a few squirts of diluted washing-up liquid.

There are so many roses to choose from (send off to growers for a catalogue or search online), but here are a handful of each type that will enhance any summer garden:

Hybrid teas

Hybrid teas are renowned for their classic, large, pointed flowers, many of which possess a delicious fragrance. They bloom on a single stem, making them ideal cut roses. They flower in June and again in September.

'Alpine Sunset' has large, fragrant yellow flowers that are flushed peach, light-green glossy leaves and good disease resistance. Height 2ft 6in. Fragrance 8.

'**Deep Secret**' is a velvety dark red with an outstanding fragrance, dark-green leaves and good disease resistance. Free flowering. Height 4ft. Fragrance 10.

'**Double Delight**' is an interesting bicolour, producing large, strongly scented blooms of cream with prominent deep-pink margins set off against glossy green foliage. Height 3ft. Fragrance 9.

'**Dutch Gold**' has fragrant, golden-yellow flowers that do not fade with age, and dark-green foliage. Height 3ft. Fragrance 8.

'**Elizabeth Harkness**' has perfectly shaped blooms that are an interesting pale-buff colour with a salmon-pink blush, and glossy, dark-green leaves. Height 2ft 6in. Fragrance 6.

'**Ice Cream**' has fragrant white flowers tinted yellow that look impressive against the bronze-green foliage. Height 3ft. Fragrance 8.

'**Just Joey**' is a popular variety with unusual ruffled blooms that are coppery-orange in colour and are freely produced against dark-green foliage. Height 2ft 6in. Fragrance 6.

'**Paul Shirville**' is an elegantly shaped, fragrant rose that has pink outer petals turning to a peachy-salmon at the centre. Height 3ft. Free flowering with dark foliage. Fragrance 8.

'**Tequila Sunrise**' has buds of scarlet and gold that open to yellow edged red, like a picotee. A real showstopper with dark, glossy leaves. Height 2ft 6in. Fragrance 5.

'**Troika**' has fragrant, coppery-orange blooms that are tinged with pink, next to glossy green, healthy foliage. Free flowering. Height 3ft. Fragrance 7.

'**Wendy Cussons**' has shapely, cerise-pink blooms with a strong fragrance. These are produced over a long period. Healthy, glossy foliage. Height 3ft. Fragrance 9.

Floribundas

Floribunda roses produce masses of slightly smaller blooms in large sprays carried over a long period from June to September. Recently introduced varieties have improved flower shape and fragrance, making them more like hybrid teas but with a greater profusion of flowers.

'Amber Queen' has open, deep-amber flowers and dark-green foliage. Height 2ft 6in. Fragrance 6.

'Champagne Moment' has large blooms with a dark apricot centre fading to creamy-white on the outer petals. Good disease resistance and glossy foliage. Height 3ft. Fragrance 7.

'Cream Abundance' produces beautifully shaped, scented cream flowers in great numbers. Foliage is dark green. Height 3ft. Fragrance 5.

'English Miss' is a free-flowering rose with shapely, fragrant, shell-pink blooms set against dark-green leaves. Height 2ft 6in. Fragrance 9.

'Eyes For You' is a new, compact variety that has open, pale-pink flowers with distinctive maroon blotches in the centres. It prefers a partially shaded spot to full sun. Height 2ft. Fragrance 9.

'Fragrant Delight' has salmon-pink flowers tinged with orange and attractive, reddish-green foliage. Height 3ft. Fragrance 8.

'Korresia' is a short variety with sunshine-yellow flowers which, although not long lasting, are produced in good numbers and have an excellent fragrance for a yellow rose. Height 2ft. Fragrance 8.

'Margaret Merril' is an exceptional white rose with a delicate pink centre, the blooms set against dark-green leaves. It has a lovely, hybrid-tea-style shape and a beautiful fragrance. Height 2ft 6in. Fragrance 10.

'Oranges and Lemons' is an interesting striped rose, producing large blooms of bright orange striped yellow. It might not be to everyone's taste but is worth growing if you are looking for something different. The young growth is red. Height 4ft. Fragrance 3.

'Rhapsody in Blue' is about as close as any grower has got to a blue rose. Its strongly fragrant, semi-double, rich purple-mauve flowers fade to slate blue and are produced in great numbers. The colour is even more pronounced in the evening, so it works well planted in partial shade. Height 3ft. Fragrance 10.

'**Tatton**' produces an abundance of fragrant, burnt-orange flowers, complemented by dark-green foliage. Height 3ft. Fragrance 8.

English roses

Bred by David Austin, English roses combine the finest qualities of hybrid teas, floribundas and classic old roses. Their large, often rosette-shaped flowers are stunning enough in their own right but blend in beautifully with herbaceous perennials in a mixed border. They bloom in June and again in September.

'**Boscobel**' has rich pink, rosette-shaped flowers flushed with salmon at the centre. It is a shorter variety than many Austin roses, making it useful even for a small border. Height 2ft 6in. Fragrance 6.

'**Charlotte**' has yellow central petals fading to white at the edges of the rosette, giving the overall effect of a gentle primrose-yellow. Height 3ft 6in. Fragrance 3.

'**Crocus Rose**' is a free-flowering rose that produces elegant, creamy-white flowers with soft apricot at the centre of the rosette. Remove side buds for better blooms. The young shoots are dark red. Height 4ft. Fragrance 3.

'**Gentle Hermione**' carries superbly fragrant, shell-pink rosettes that fade slightly towards the outside. A reliable, rain-resistant variety. Height 4ft. Fragrance 9.

'**Munstead Wood**' has exactly the strength of fragrance expected of a dark-red rose, and its large rosettes are surrounded by healthy foliage that is red-bronze when young before turning green. Height 3ft. Fragrance 10.

'**Pat Austin**' has striking copper-yellow, cup-shaped flowers that glow a brilliant orange in the sun. It has healthy green foliage and is a prolific flowerer, blooming non-stop from June to September. Height 4ft. Fragrance 4.

'**Rosemoor**' bears medium-sized rosettes that are a delicate soft pink with a darker centre. Height 4ft. Fragrance 7.

'**Tea Clipper**' produces large rosettes that are apricot in the centre, fading to creamy-white on the outer petals. Eventually the entire flower turns creamy-white. Its height makes it a good rose for the back of a border. Height 4ft 6in. Fragrance 5.

'**Tradescant**' is a compact variety with relatively small, fragrant, deep-velvety-red flowers. Height 2ft 6in. Fragrance 9.

'**William Shakespeare**' has large, shapely, red rosettes that are neither as dark nor as fragrant as 'Munstead Wood', although the fragrance improves as the season progresses. Height 4ft. Fragrance 7.

'**Young Lycidas**' bears large, richly fragrant, cupped, cerise-pink flowers on arching stems almost non-stop from June to September. The young growth is red. Height 3ft 6in. Fragrance 10.

Old roses

Old roses may lack the colour range of modern varieties and many bloom only in the summer, but they usually have a wonderful fragrance.

'**Alba Maxima**' is a popular old variety that produces double, fragrant, creamy-white flowers in summer. Height 6ft. Fragrance 8.

'**Cardinal de Richelieu**' is a gallica rose with double flowers that are almost purple. It is almost thornless but flowers in summer only. Height 5ft. Fragrance 6.

'**Charles de Mills**' is a fragrant gallica rose that produces large, double flowers of a deep magenta-crimson with hints of purple during mid-summer. It has dark-green foliage and good disease resistance. Height 4ft. Fragrance 8.

'**Comte de Chambord**' is a repeat-flowering Portland rose that bears very fragrant, full-pink flowers on a tough and healthy bush. Height 4ft. Fragrance 9.

'**Ferdinand Pichard**' produces distinctive, globular, pink flowers that are striped with crimson. It has a lovely fragrance and repeat flowers, although the autumn flush is rarely as good as the first. Height 4ft. Fragrance 8.

'**Rose de Rescht**' is a healthy, repeat-flowering Portland rose with double, fragrant, deep-pink flowers on a compact bush, making it suitable for a smaller garden. Height 3ft. Fragrance 9.

Shrub roses

Shrub roses are generally larger and bushier than hybrid teas, floribundas and English roses, but with smaller flowers, and many bloom once only, albeit for a long period.

'**Blush Noisette**' bears clusters of semi-double, blush-pink flowers that are produced through summer and into autumn. The flowers have a distinctive clove scent and the foliage is dark green and healthy. Height 6ft. Fragrance 7.

'**Buff Beauty**' is a vigorous plant that from mid-summer bears trusses of semi-double, apricot flowers that fade to buff-yellow on the outer petals. Height 5ft. Fragrance 5.

'**Cerise Bouquet**' is a shrub rose bearing neat, semi-double, cerise-pink flowers on long, arching stems in summer. Height 9ft. Fragrance 2.

'**Frühlingsgold**' has large, pale-yellow, almost single flowers with darker yellow stamens from mid-summer. Height 7ft. Fragrance 5.

Rosa rugosa '**Alba**' is a wild rose carrying large, richly fragrant, single, white flowers with prominent yellow stamens over a long period from July to September. The flowers are followed by eye-catching, orange-red hips. *R. rugosa* '**Rubra**' is similar but with deep-pink flowers. Both grow to a height of 6ft and make excellent hedges, offering a thorny barrier and filling the air with their scent. Fragrance 10.

Miniature and patio roses

Miniature and patio roses are useful for growing in containers or on a rock garden. Miniatures have small leaves and flowers, while patio roses have larger, floribunda-sized flowers but on more compact bushes. Both flower over a long period through summer and into autumn.

'Baby Masquerade' is a miniature version of a popular floribunda rose famed for its ability to produce yellow, pink and red flowers simultaneously on the same bush. Height 18in. Fragrance 1.

'Cream Dream' is a bushy patio rose that is smothered in neatly cupped flowers that have amber-yellow centres fading to creamy-white outer petals. Height 18in. Fragrance 1.

'Dream Lover' is a rarity: a miniature rose with perfume. It has pretty, lilac, rosette-shaped flowers that are produced profusely and over a long period. Height 18in. Fragrance 8.

'Hand in Hand' is a free-flowering patio rose with shapely vermillion-red flowers. Height 2ft. Fragrance 1.

'Mr Bluebird' produces small, semi-double flowers that are magenta-mauve with a white eye. Height 1ft. Fragrance 1.

'Stars 'n' Stripes' has small flowers with red-and-white stripes, like a baby 'Ferdinand Pichard' but without the fragrance. Height 1ft. Fragrance 1.

'Sweet Dream' is similar to 'Cream Dream' but with flowers that are an attractive salmon-pink. Height 18in. Fragrance 1.

'The Fairy' bears masses of soft pink, rosette-shaped flowers on a neat little bush. Height 2ft. Fragrance 1.

'Violet Cloud' is a novel patio rose that has single, lilac-mauve flowers with a white eye and yellow stamens. Height 2ft. Fragrance 4.

Groundcover roses

A few varieties of rose make good groundcover plants.

'Grouse 2000' is a repeat-flowering variety that forms a carpet of single, white flowers with yellow stamens. Height 2ft, spread 3ft. Fragrance 5.

'Scented Carpet' has small, single, fragrant, lilac-pink flowers and healthy, glossy foliage on arching, spreading stems. Height 2ft, spread 4ft. Fragrance 8.

'**Suffolk**' is covered in single, scarlet flowers with prominent yellow stamens, succeeded by orange hips. Repeat flowering. Height 18in, spread 3ft. Fragrance 1.

Likes Any soil in a sunny spot.

Flowering season June–September.

Key points Stunning colour and fragrance, most varieties repeat flower. Attractive leaves, lovely cut flowers.

VFM 10

Sambucus nigra f. porphyrophylla (Purple-leaved Elder)

The purple-leaved elder is a good choice for a new garden because it allows you to fill a large space in a short time with a tough, hardy, deciduous shrub whose dark-purple, almost black, leaves contrast beautifully not only with its pink flowers but also with any golden-leaved shrubs. The new leaves are actually dark green but soon turn almost black before changing to rich red in autumn. They are so deeply dissected that they resemble lace, hence the name of one of the most popular cultivars, *S. nigra f. porphyrophylla* **'Black Lace'**.

To obtain the best foliage colour, plant it in full sun. The flat flower heads are a pretty, soft pink and have a pleasant musk scent. These appear in May and are followed by black berries, which are edible and can be turned into wine. A tasty cordial can also be made from the flowers. Unpruned, it will reach a height of nearly 20ft, but to keep it more compact and to promote larger and more colourful leaves, cut it back hard in late winter. It will grow anywhere – even in waterlogged ground or dry, chalky soil – and at a rapid pace. If black-fly prove a nuisance on the black shoots, spray them with diluted washing-up liquid. Other fine cultivars include *S. nigra f. porphyrophylla* **'Black Beauty'** and *S. nigra f. porphyrophylla* **'Guincho Purple'.** You could try planting the purple-leaved elder next to *S. nigra* **'Aurea'**, the golden elder, which has golden-yellow leaves and clusters of white flowers.

Likes Any soil in a sunny spot.

Flowering season May–June.

Key points Black leaves contrast with pink flowers and turn red in autumn. Edible black berries, easy to grow, fast growing.

VFM 8

Spiraea japonica 'Goldflame'

This neat little deciduous shrub offers a 'traffic-light' foliage display during the course of the summer. The young leaves are a striking bronze-gold colour before turning red, bright yellow and finally a glowing green. From July these are supported by flat heads composed of numerous tiny dark-pink flowers. It is an easy shrub to grow, provided you give it a sunny location and it has soil that drains well but retains some moisture. If your ground is on the heavy side, add plenty of horticultural grit at planting time, along with rotted compost – and remember to mulch in the spring when the new growth is coming through. *S. japonica* **'Goldflame'** forms a compact shape with a height and spread of 3ft, making it suitable for a large rock garden or the front of a shrub border. For the best foliage colour, every spring cut the stems back to a framework about 6in above the ground.

Likes Well-drained, moisture-retentive soil in full sun.
Flowering season July–August.
Key points Foliage is bronze-gold when young before turning red, bright yellow and then green. Pink flowers. Neat, compact shrub.
VFM 8

Symphoricarpos (Snowberry)

Although it produces dainty flowers in the summer, the deciduous snowberry is grown primarily for its white, pink or purple, marble-like berries that first appear around October and last well into winter, long after the shrub has shed its leaves. These berries can cause a mild skin irritation, so wear gloves when you are handling the plant. Most forms grow to a height of around 6ft and will thrive just about anywhere, except on waterlogged ground.

They take poor soil, urban pollution and strong winds in their stride and are reliable performers for sites where fussier shrubs may struggle, such as beneath trees. They cope with partial shade as well as full sun and require little pruning apart from the removal of any dead branches. However, if you decide to grow snowberry as a hedge, you will need to cut back the flowered shoots immediately after flowering to maintain shape and encourage lateral growth.

S. albus var. laevigatus is a fast-growing, sturdy shrub with dense, dark-green foliage. It has small pink flowers in summer followed by a profusion of white berries that often last right through winter. Height and spread 6ft.

S. chenaultii **'Hancock'** produces tiny white flowers in late summer followed by purple-pink berries. Height and spread 6ft.

S. doorenbosii **'Magic Berry'** is a compact shrub with dark-green leaves that turn dull yellow in autumn, and pale-pink flowers followed by clusters of rose-pink berries. Height and spread 4ft.

S. doorenbosii **'Mother of Pearl'** is a tough, fast-growing shrub with small white flowers and an abundance of white berries that are heavily flushed rose-pink. Height and spread 8ft.

S. orbiculatus has dark-green leaves, white flowers flushed with pink, and dark-purple berries. Height and spread 5ft. *S. orbiculatus* **'Foliis Variegatis'** is similar but with mid-green leaves that are edged yellow.

Likes Any reasonably drained soil in sun or partial shade.

Flowering season July–August.

Key points Summer flowers followed by white, pink or purple berries in autumn and winter. Easy to grow.

VFM 7

Vinca (Periwinkle)

A lot of gardens have an awkward area of shade where the only things that seem to want to grow are weeds. To suppress these you need a fast-growing, tough groundcover plant – and they don't come much tougher than periwinkle. The most vigorous species, *Vinca major* (greater periwinkle), loves a shady location provided it does not become too dry and will quickly cover a wide expanse, forming a low carpet of shiny, evergreen leaves topped by large, 2in-wide, violet-blue flowers that appear from spring right through until early autumn.

One cultivar, *V. major* **'Variegata'** (aka **'Elegantissima'**), has the bonus of variegated leaves that are dark green with creamy-white margins, creating a welcome splash of colour in winter. The creeping stems reach a height of about 18in but will spread to cover an area of 50 sq ft or more. If it becomes too invasive, simply cut back any surplus shoots in spring to show it who's boss. As you might expect from its name, *Vinca minor* (lesser periwinkle) is not as aggressive, growing to about half the size of its big brother and therefore a useful groundcover plant for a smaller space. It also prefers more sun than *V. major* but still tolerates partial shade. *V. minor* **'Argenteovariegata'** bears violet-blue flowers over many months and these are backed by greyish-green leaves with creamy-white edges. *V. minor* **'Atropurpurea'** produces dark-green leaves and lovely plum-purple flowers. *V. minor f. alba* **'Gertrude Jekyll'** is even more compact, only spreading to about 18in, and its dark-green leaves contrast nicely with its snowy-white flowers.

Likes Any reasonable soil in a fairly shady spot.
Flowering season April–September.
Key points Evergreen groundcover plant with violet-blue, plum-purple or white flowers carried over a long period. Some varieties have variegated leaves. Easy to grow, low maintenance.
VFM 8

Weigela

Weigelas are among the most aristocratic of deciduous shrubs, their branches smothered in a wealth of pink, ruby-red, white or yellow funnel-shaped flowers in late spring, invariably set against a backdrop of variegated, golden or plum-coloured foliage. Some species are slow growing while others will reach a height and spread of 8ft in no time. All are remarkably accommodating provided you give them a fairly sunny spot, although the golden-leaved varieties do prefer some shade. They will thrive in any soil, but add plenty of rotted compost or farmyard manure when planting to get them off to a good start.

Maintenance is minimal. You can just let your weigela do its own thing and not bother with any pruning, but if you want to control its spread trim back the branches on established plants by up to a third immediately after flowering. At the same time, you can remove some of the really old branches altogether.

W. **'Boskoop Glory'** produces satin-pink flowers and mid-green leaves. Height and spread 5ft.

W. **'Bristol Ruby'** is a fast-growing shrub with deep ruby-red flowers and dark-green leaves that are flushed purple when young. Height and spread 5ft.

W. **'Ebony and Ivory'** is a new, compact plant whose red-throated, white flowers contrast splendidly with the dark-green leaves that become flushed with plum as they age. Height 2ft, spread 3ft.

W. florida **'Foliis Purpureis'** is a compact shrub with clusters of dark-pink flowers emerging from carmine-red buds and purple-green leaves whose colour is more pronounced in full sun. Height 3ft, spread 5ft. *W.* **'Florida Variegata'** is just about the best variegated shrub you can buy. In late spring it produces hundreds of two-tone pink flowers that emerge from dark-pink buds. These flowers are borne on elegant, arching branches laden with large, white-edged, grey-green leaves. Fast growing. Height and spread 8ft. For a smaller garden there is a dwarf cultivar, *W. florida* **'Monet'**

('**Verweig**'), which has pink flowers and green-and-white variegated leaves that are tinged with pink, and only reaches a height and spread of 2ft.

W. looymansii '**Aurea**' has pale-pink flowers and golden-yellow leaves. It is best grown in partial shade to prevent leaf scorch. Height and spread 5ft.

W. middendorffiana '**Mango**' is a striking new variety that has sulphur-yellow flowers, each with a mottled orange-pink throat. The leaves are a lush green. Height 4ft, spread 3ft.

W. '**Mont Blanc**' is a vigorous shrub that produces large, fragrant, white flowers flushed with pink, along with dark-green leaves. Height and spread 5ft.

Likes Any reasonable soil in sun or partial shade.
Flowering season May–June.
Key points Magnificent flowers and colourful leaves. Easy to grow, long-lived.
VFM 9

PART VIII

Climbers

Bare walls and fences are often the least attractive parts of a garden – a stark reminder of where your patch of land ends. However, if you conceal and soften the barren brickwork or plain panels with attractive climbing plants, the garden suddenly acquires a natural, vertical extension. Climbers can also be used for adorning pergolas and arches and for growing up through large shrubs or trees, where they serve to prolong the season of interest. Even if you have no soil next to a wall or fence, you can still grow some climbers by planting them in large containers.

Species such as ivy and Virginia creeper use suckers to attach themselves to surfaces, so they need no additional assistance, but climbing roses and clematis will need a framework of wires in order that the stems can be tied and trained to the desired shape. This does not have to be a great chore. Simply insert two screws or nails into the fence or wall about 5ft apart and just a few inches above the top of the plant. Tie the wire around both screws or nails until it is taut and, if necessary, tighten the screws. Repeat the process at least twice more, progressing higher up the fence, so that you end up with at least three horizontal, 5ft-long wires at height intervals of 1ft. As the plant grows, use garden twine to tie the shoots to the wire framework. Alternatively, you can buy a large, ready-made, wooden trellis for attaching to a fence or wall.

Of all popular climbing plants, clematis offer the widest range of colours, but they are not without their challenges and sadly their mortality rate is just too high for them to be included in this book. Fortunately, there are some less demanding climbers.

Hedera (Ivy)

Ivy can be either a curse or a blessing to gardeners: a curse because it has a habit of popping up unexpectedly where you least want it, having self-seeded from neighbours' plots, and a blessing because its evergreen leaves – particularly the variegated forms – are ideal for hiding an unsightly wall or fence, even in the depths of winter. Ivy can grow so dense that robins and wrens often choose to nest in it, and because it is self clinging by virtue of aerial roots and suckers attached to the creeping stems, it needs no artificial framework to aid its spread. However, it is such an effective climber that over a prolonged period it can wreck guttering and seriously damage the mortar in between brickwork, so it is best not to let it scramble up the walls of the house. Wherever you choose to grow ivy, don't let it run riot; keep it under some form of control by cutting back unwanted stems at any time of year.

Ivies prefer moist but well-drained soil, so add some horticultural grit at planting time if you garden on heavy clay. Like all shrubs, they will also appreciate a helping of garden compost or manure. They will grow anywhere from full sun to deep shade, although the variegated forms may lose their colour if grown in too much shade. The common English ivy is *Hedera helix*, which has insignificant yellow-green flowers in late autumn, but the berries that follow are much loved by birds. There are a number of attractive forms, along with a few other hardy species that are suitable for the garden.

H. colchica **'Dentata'** – the Persian ivy – is a hardy, vigorous climber that has large, heart-shaped, glossy green leaves and stems that are tinged with purple. It produces large, green flowers in late autumn, followed by black berries in winter. It likes partial to deep shade and in ten years can reach a height of 30ft and a spread of 12ft, so it is not a plant for a small garden unless you are prepared to be ruthless from time to time. For a sunnier spot, choose *H. colchica* **'Dentata Variegata'**, whose leaves have broad, creamy-yellow margins.

H. helix **'Atropurpurea'**– the purple-leaved ivy – will grow anywhere and has medium-sized, dark-green leaves that turn very dark purple in cold weather, making it a good plant for winter foliage. If left unchecked, in ten years it can reach a height of 25ft and a spread of 10ft. *H. helix* **'Buttercup'** is a better subject for a small garden, growing to a height of only 8ft and a spread of 5ft. It carries broad, bright-yellow leaves, although these will revert to light green in shade. *H. helix* **'Glacier'** has grey-green leaves with irregular, creamy margins and reaches a height and spread of 6ft. As with all variegated forms, it is best grown in sun for full leaf colour. *H. helix* **'Ivalace'** is a dwarf cultivar that only reaches a height of 3ft and a spread of 2ft. It has dark, glossy green leaves with attractive veining and crisped edges, and although it has no flowers it will grow happily in sun or shade.

H. hibernica – Atlantic or Irish ivy – is a good plant if you want to cover a large wall quickly. It has glossy, dark-green leaves, prefers partial to deep shade and has a vigorous habit. It produces white flowers in autumn followed by clusters of dark-blue berries. Eventual height 30ft, spread 25ft.

Likes Moist, well-drained soil in sun or shade.

Flowering season October–November.

Key points Evergreen for year-round interest, pretty, variegated forms. Self clinging, so needs no framework. Winter berries attract birds.

VFM 8

Jasminum nudiflorum (Winter Jasmine)

In the dark winter months, there are few cheerier sights in the garden than the golden-yellow flowers of winter jasmine scrambling up a trellis or wall. Technically it is not a climber – even though that tends to be its chief role in the garden – and therefore the growing stems need tying to a framework at every stage. This is easily done as the stems are sturdy but pliable and can be trained with the minimum of fuss. It is a deciduous shrub, and so the flowers are produced on bare stems, but the latter retain their bright-green colour throughout winter in support of the blooms. When the dark-green leaves appear, they are small and unobtrusive.

Winter jasmine is tolerant of all soils, but it does require decent drainage, so if you garden on heavy clay add horticultural grit along with rotted compost or leaf mould when planting. It prefers full sun but can also cope with partial shade. It is a vigorous plant and can eventually reach a height and spread of 12ft. It is not a shrub that insists on being pruned annually, but to encourage new growth you can prune the shoots that have borne flowers back to strong side shoots in March. It is important not to leave pruning until later in the year because then you risk removing the branches on which the following year's flowers are forming. March is also a good time to remove any weak or overcrowded stems. If your mature winter jasmine gets far too big for its space, don't be afraid to cut the plant back hard to just 2ft above the ground. It will grow again with renewed vigour, although it will take a couple of years to flower. The only downside with winter jasmine is that, unlike other, less hardy, jasmines, the flowers are not scented.

Likes Well-drained soil in full sun or partial shade.
Flowering season November–February.
Key points Yellow flowers and green stems for winter interest. Hardy, vigorous, easy to train.
VFM 8

Parthenocissus quinquefolia (Virginia Creeper)

Virginia creeper is the quintessential autumn foliage plant, capable of turning an entire wall into a mass of red, orange and burgundy. In full flow it is a truly spectacular sight, but it requires plenty of room to be seen at its best as it can reach a height of 50ft and a spread of 20ft and will grow up to 10ft in a single year. Like ivy, it is a self-clinging plant that needs no wire support, but if left to rampage too freely it can damage guttering, so if you are planting it on a house wall you will need to prune it from time to time. It will swamp everything in its path, so similarly you will need to train it around any windows, alarms and so on. It is also a good idea to check the wall beforehand for any obvious cracks, because the shoots can get in and cause problems.

Having dealt with its potential powers of destruction, let's focus on the positives. Virginia creeper will grow anywhere – in full sun or in deep shade – but for the best display, plant it where it receives plenty of sun, so ideally not on a north-facing wall. It thrives in any soil – moist or dry, clay or chalk – and is even salt tolerant, making it suitable for coastal gardens. Before you know it, that bare, unlovely wall will be transformed in spring by a lush layer of large, five-lobed, mid-green leaves, which change colour all through summer to dark green and pink, culminating in the fiery reds and oranges of autumn. It also produces small, yellow-green flowers in early summer, followed by blue-black berries, which are poisonous to humans but harmless to birds. Unfortunately it is deciduous, so the wall you wanted to hide away will not be concealed in winter; but all in all – provided you are willing to keep it house-trained – I would say the plant's pros definitely outweigh the cons. Who's afraid of Virginia creeper?

Likes Any soil in sun or shade.

Flowering season June–July.

Key points Rich, red and orange leaves in autumn. Blue-black berries. Fast growing, ideal for covering a wall quickly. Self clinging, so needs no support.

VFM 8

Rosa (Climbing Rose and Rambling Rose)

One of the best ways to appreciate the beauty of roses is to see large specimens climbing over a pergola or adorning a wall or fence, particularly when they are highly scented and their fragrance fills the evening air. There are two types of rose for such situations: climbers and ramblers. Climbing roses have a wider colour range, generally repeat flower and are invariably more compact, making them the better choice for a small garden. Ramblers are at their finest in large country gardens, where they can often be seen winding their way up trees. Their clusters of flowers are borne in great numbers – hundreds at a time – but often only once a year and invariably smaller in size than those on climbing roses.

Neither type is self clinging, so they will need tying into some form of framework. If being trained up a pillar or pergola, the main shoots should be gently twisted around the uprights, keeping them as horizontal as possible so that the plant produces flowers low down rather than just at the top. If designed to conceal a wall or a fence, the stems should be trained into the approximate shape of a fan so that they are spread out and not all bunched together. Using a system of horizontal wires should guarantee the production of flowers on the lower stems (and therefore crucially within sniffing range).

The basic planting method for roses has already been described in the entry for bush roses (see Shrubs, p.162), but because climbers and ramblers are bigger plants they will need extra nutrients. Also, the soil near walls and fences tends to be poor, so add generous amounts of rotted garden compost or leaf mould to the soil before planting. When it comes to pruning, ramblers can be left to get on with it. The only cutting back you really need to do is to remove any dead, diseased or tangled shoots in late summer or early autumn, usually with the aid of a ladder. Climbing roses should be pruned annually, like bush roses, in late February or early March. Cut back the previous year's flowering shoots to leave three or four strong side shoots on each branch. At the same time, remove any weak or crossed stems and tie in the strong, new ones to your framework.

Climbing roses

Here are some of the best climbing roses:

'Aloha' has large, very fragrant, salmon-pink, hybrid-tea-style blooms and glossy, dark-green leaves. It repeats well and is tough enough to cope with a north-facing wall. Height 8ft. Fragrance 9.

'Blush Noisette' boasts clusters of cup-shaped, semi-double, lilac-pink flowers with a rich clove scent and is a good repeat flowerer. It likes a warm, sunny spot in the garden. Height 8ft. Fragrance 7.

'Chris' has large, hybrid-tea-style blooms of bright yellow with orange shadings on the outer petals, fading to creamy-yellow with age. It is healthy, has a strong fragrance and repeats well. Height 8ft. Fragrance 8.

'Compassion' is one of the most popular modern climbing roses, producing a profusion of double, fragrant, salmon-pink flowers that are tinted with apricot-orange and are set against lush, dark-green leaves. It is a strong, vigorous grower and an excellent repeat flowerer. Height 10ft. Fragrance 7.

'Crimson Glory' has large, deep-red blooms with a wonderful fragrance. It blooms freely in summer with occasional flowers later. Height 15ft. Fragrance 9.

'Ena Harkness' has large, velvety-red flowers with a strong fragrance. As a hybrid tea rose, it is notorious for its weak neck, which causes every bloom to hang, but this is not such a problem in a climber. Height 15ft. Fragrance 9.

'Étoile de Hollande' produces deep-crimson, highly fragrant flowers supported by glossy, dark-green leaves. It is a vigorous, repeat flowerer. Height 12ft. Fragrance 9.

'Fashion' bears a profusion of semi-double, floribunda-style, salmon-pink flowers. Height 10ft. Fragrance 5.

'**Gloire de Dijon**' is an old cottage-garden favourite that flowers early and produces a strong second flush later in the season. The large, richly fragrant, double flowers vary considerably in colour from pale yellow to soft apricot and pink, creating a most effective display on a sunny wall. Height 15ft. Fragrance 8.

'**Golden Showers**' has large, semi-double flowers of golden-yellow fading to cream on almost thornless stems. A tough variety, it is suitable for a cold, north-facing wall and repeats well. Height 10ft. Fragrance 5.

'**Handel**' produces lightly fragrant blooms that are an interesting pink-and-cream bi-colour. Each beautifully shaped flower is creamy-yellow with a rosy-pink edging that intensifies with age. Foliage is glossy green-tinted-bronze and it is a good repeat flowerer. Height 12ft. Fragrance 6.

'**Iceberg**' is a climbing form of the popular floribunda, producing sprays of medium-sized, pure-white flowers that are occasionally tinged with pink later in the season. A good repeat flowerer. Height 10ft. Fragrance 3.

'**Josephine Bruce**' bears large, highly scented, dark-red, hybrid tea blooms on a vigorous bush. Height 15ft. Fragrance 9.

'**Lady Hillingdon**' combines shapely, fragrant, apricot flowers with plum-coloured shoots and dark-green foliage. It is a fast grower and flowers freely throughout the summer. Height 15ft. Fragrance 7.

'**Mme. Alfred Carrière**' is an old variety with large, sweetly scented, double flowers that are white, sometimes flushed with soft pink. A strong grower, it blooms freely and continuously – often for months on end. Height 20ft. Fragrance 8.

'**Maigold**' has large, fragrant, semi-double, coppery-yellow flowers and a mass of glossy, green foliage. Exceptionally tough, it produces an abundance of blooms in summer followed by a small repeat display in September. Height 12ft. Fragrance 7.

'**New Dawn**' has long been a garden favourite, producing sprays of elegant, fragrant, 3in-wide, shell-pink flowers and plenty of glossy foliage. It blooms freely from early summer to late autumn. Height 10ft. Fragrance 6.

'Parade' boasts double, fragrant, cerise-pink flowers and healthy, glossy foliage over a long period. Height 10ft. Fragrance 5.

'Schoolgirl' has large, fragrant, hybrid-tea-shape flowers of coppery-orange that are produced repeatedly through summer and into autumn. Foliage is abundant and glossy. Height 10ft. Fragrance 6.

'Summertime' is a climbing patio rose that produces masses of small, fragrant, double, yellow flowers from top to bottom and from late spring until autumn. It is suitable for growing in a container as well as in the more traditional manner. Height 7ft. Fragrance 4.

'Warm Welcome' is another new climbing patio rose that is a great variety for a smaller garden. Its vibrant, orange, semi-double flowers are produced from June until the first frosts. Height 6ft. Fragrance 2.

Rambling roses

Here are some of the choicest rambling roses:

'Albéric Barbier' is a classic variety bearing clusters of double, creamy-white, slightly fragrant flowers that open from yellow buds. It has lovely, glossy foliage and, unusually for a rambler, often produces a second display of flowers after the main show in June. Height 25ft. Fragrance 5.

'Albertine' is another old favourite, producing large, pink, semi-double flowers with a fabulous fragrance. A free-flowering, vigorous variety, it is excellent for trailing over an arch or pergola. Height 20ft. Fragrance 9.

'Bleu Magenta' is an almost thornless, mid-summer variety with masses of double, violet-purple, lightly scented flowers amongst glossy foliage. Height 15ft. Fragrance 5.

'Crimson Shower' has double, bright-red flowers set against dark, glossy foliage. It starts flowering in mid summer and contin-ues into September. Height 12ft. Fragrance 3.

'Francis E. Lester' bears hundreds of small, single, highly fragrant blooms that are white tinted with pink at the edges, the petals contrasting with the prominent yellow stamens. It produces small orange hips in the autumn. Height 15ft. Fragrance 7.

'Paul's Himalayan Musk' has pretty, dainty sprays of richly fragrant, pale-pink, rosette-shaped flowers that darken towards the centre. It only flowers once a year, but its display is outstanding – a great variety for covering pergolas, buildings or trees. Height 30ft. Fragrance 8.

'Princess Louise' bears sprays of fragrant, double, lilac-pink flowers with creamy-white shading. A good rambling rose for a relatively limited space. Height 12ft. Fragrance 7.

'Veilchenblau' carries bunches of small, orange-scented, semi-double flowers that open a dark magenta colour streaked with white before fading to lilac-blue. The flowers are set against attractive light-green leaves on thornless stems. Height 15ft. Fragrance 6.

'Wedding Day' has masses of single, fragrant, creamy-white flowers that are sometimes flushed pink. Its glossy foliage and vigorous growth make it a good variety for training up a tree. Height 30ft. Fragrance 7.

Likes Fertile, moisture-retentive soil in full sun.
Flowering season June–July, September (climbers); June–July (ramblers).
Key points Magnificent flowers, many with strong fragrance. Perfect for creating that cottage-garden look.
VFM 10

Index